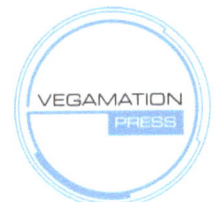

VEGAMATION
PRESS

www.vegamationpress.com

Your source for art books from breakthrough artists

INTRO DUCING

...

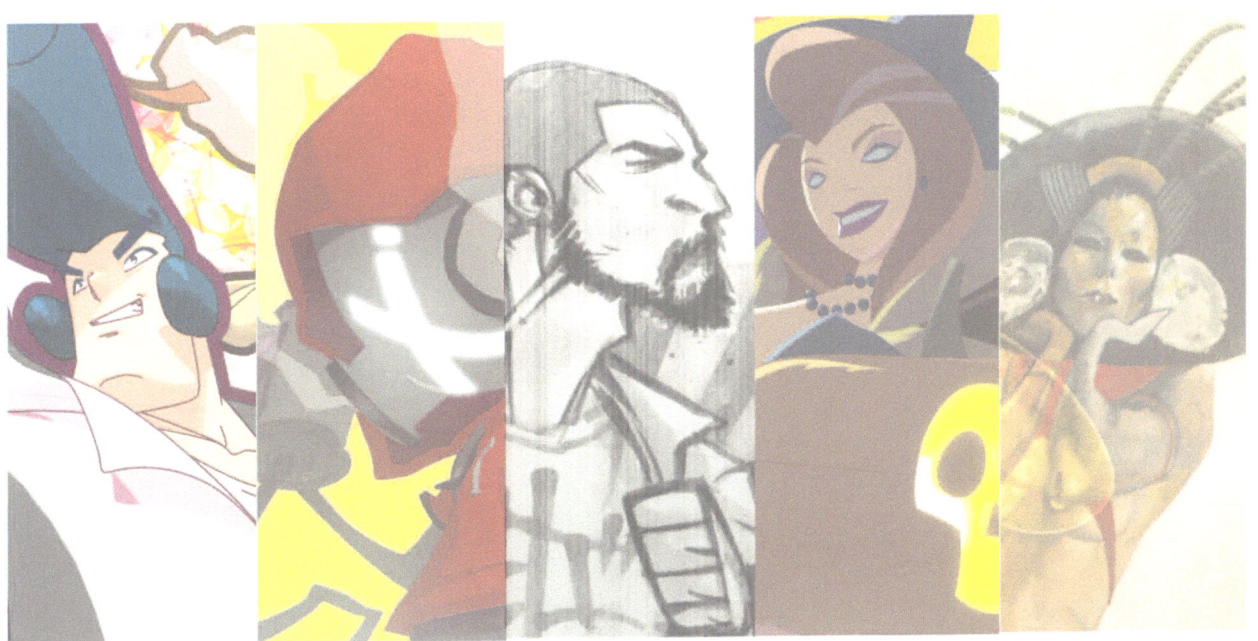

These artists were specifically chosen for their talents in this age of the Neo Kulture.

What is Neo Kulture?

Neo Kulture is a movement, your movement. Artists today have culture, music, animation, comics, films and video games interwoven in their creative threads so that it spills into their reality. Spoken aloud or not, this is a major influence in our culture...the Neo Kulture.

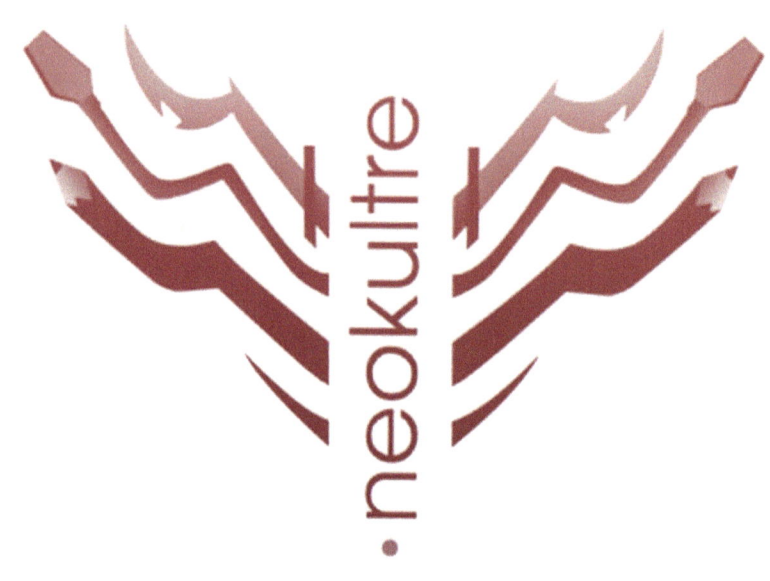

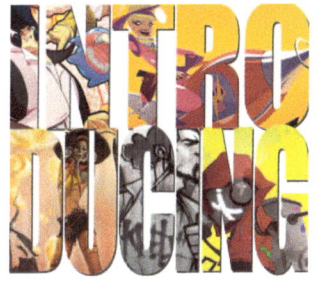

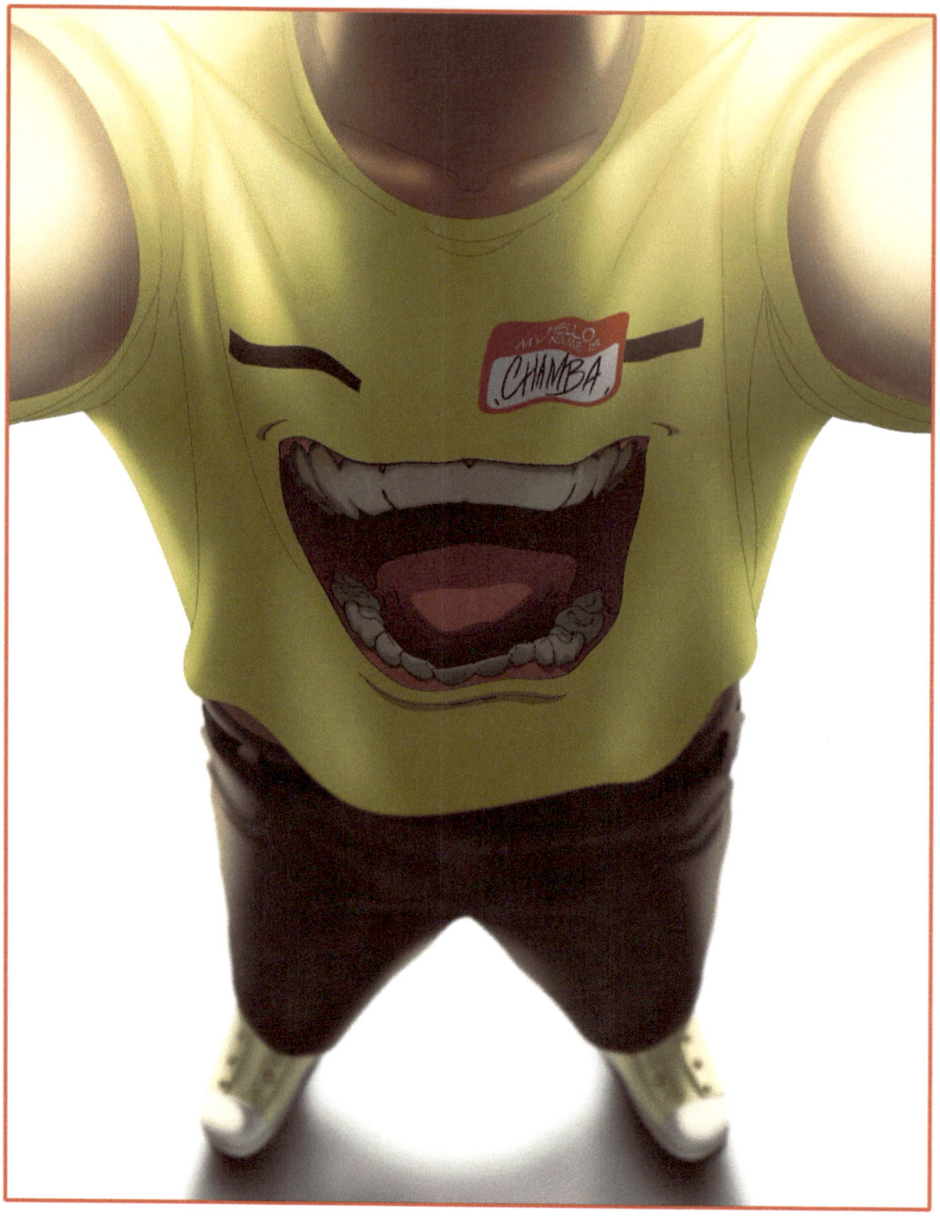

jeffCRUZ *aka* Chamba

Jeffrey Cruz (known also by his pen name of Chamba) is a man of few things to say of himself.

Since as early as '89 the year he first consciously picked up a pencil, he's had one main constant in his life. That constant being his love of Art and his unending passion to simply draw. With an unused Bachelor's degree in Art under his belt, he has somehow managed to land several illustrating gigs here and there, all thanks to his UDON connection.

A resident of Melbourne, Australia, he hopes to continue living his passion of art for as long as he can. Other loves include wicked anime/manga, delicious pizza (deep dish, YUMMM!) and soundtrack music.

Contact: web www.chamba-lang-ito.blogspot.com   e-mail jeffrey.chamba.cruz@gmail.com

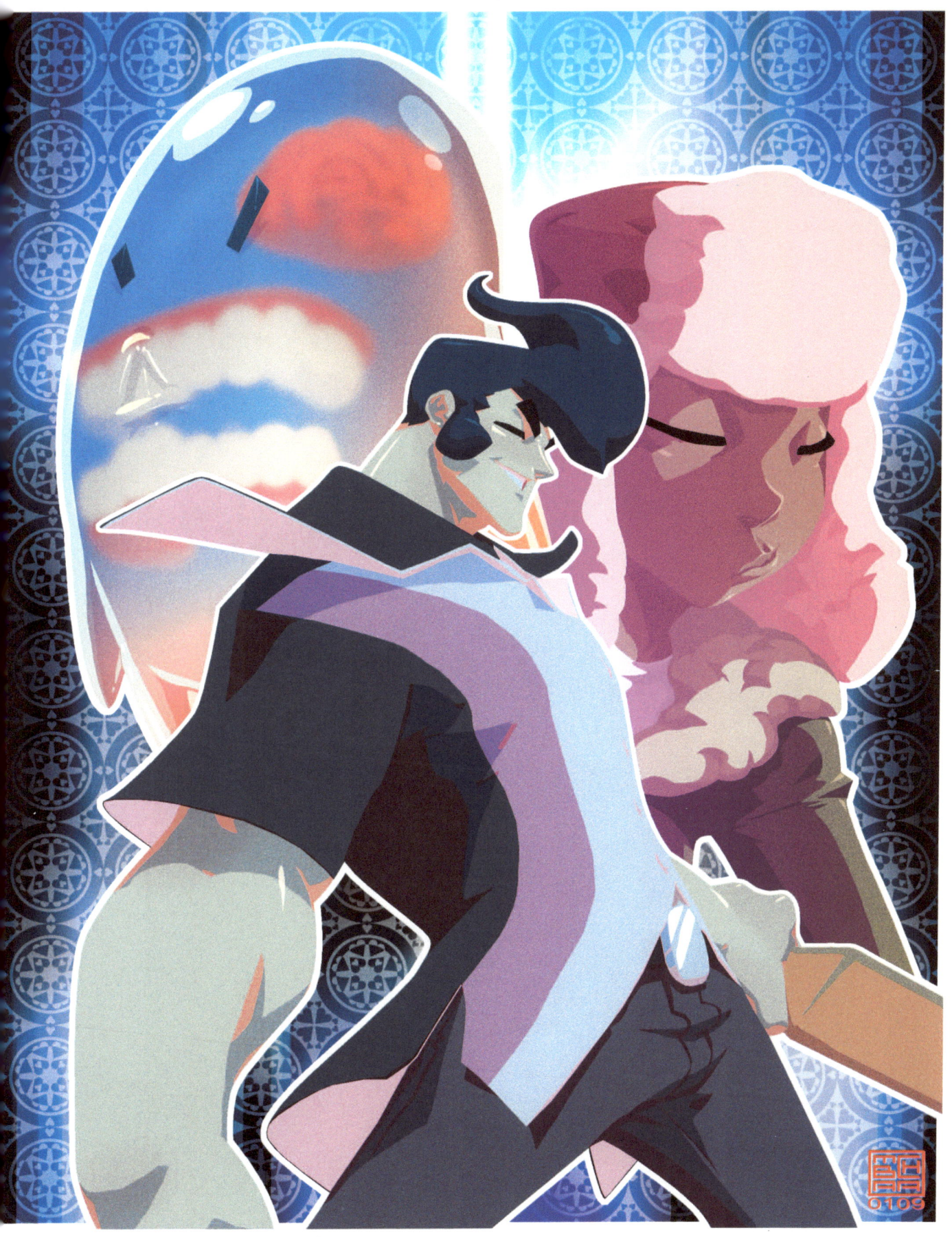

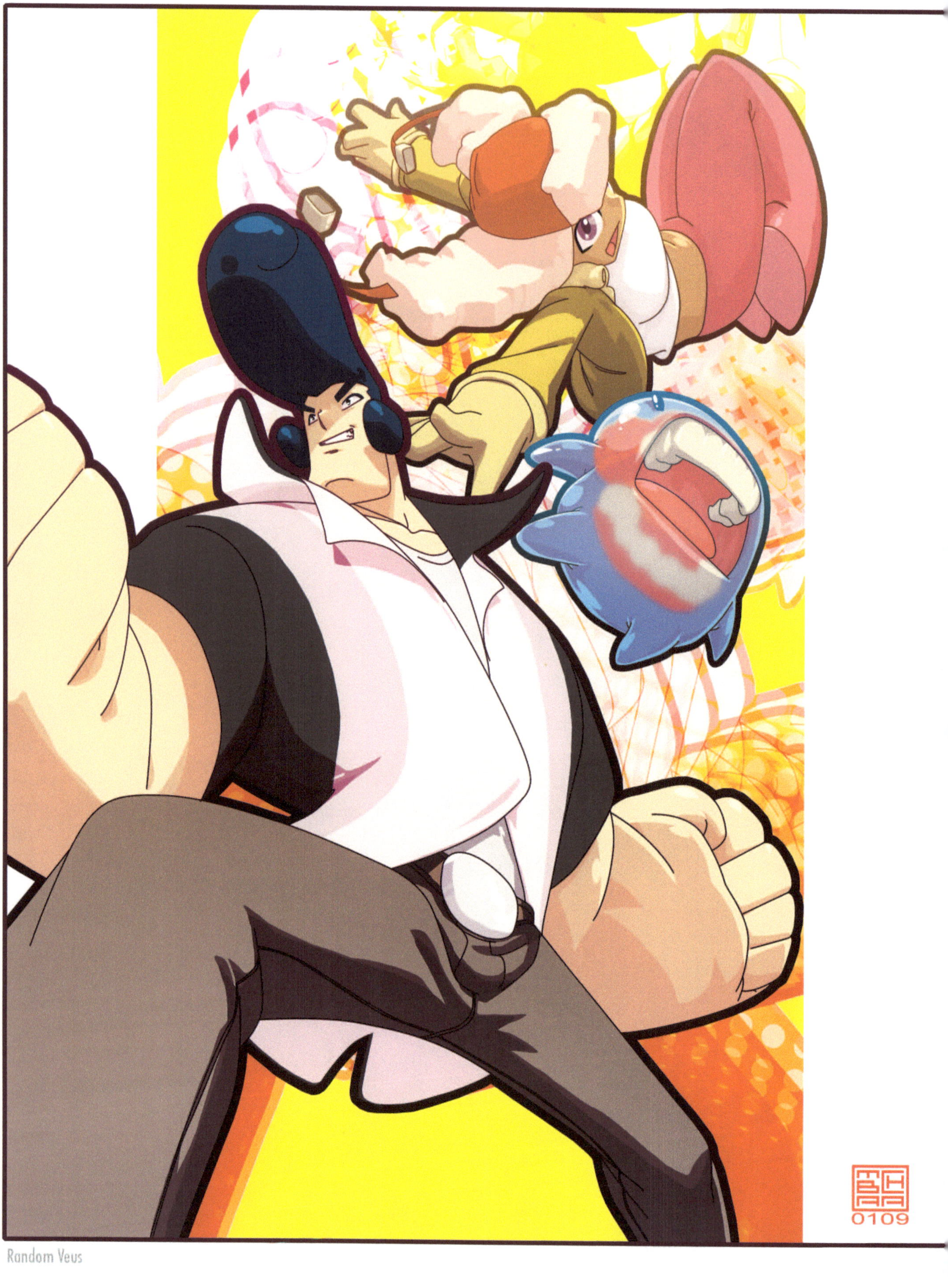

Random Veus

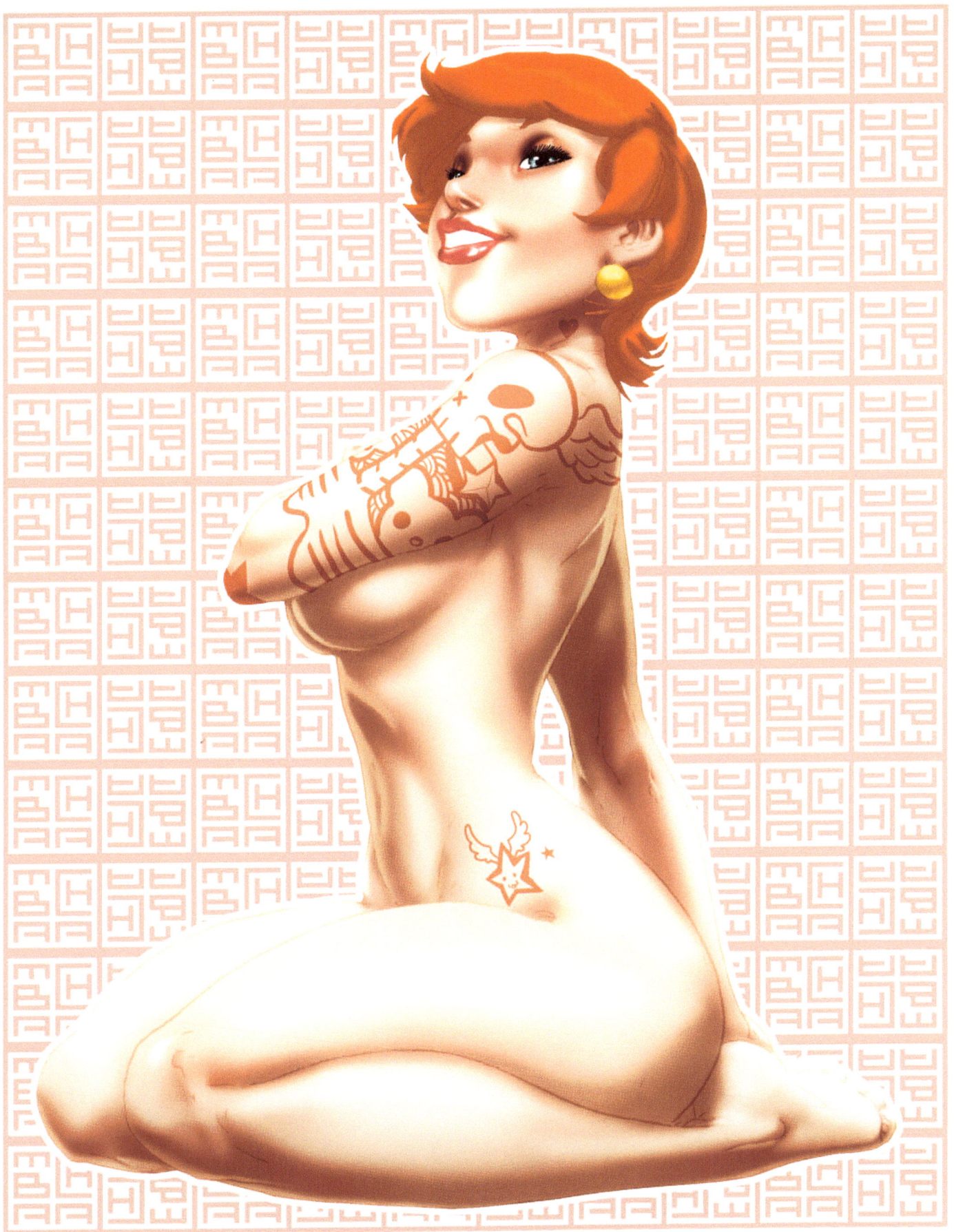

ChickaONE

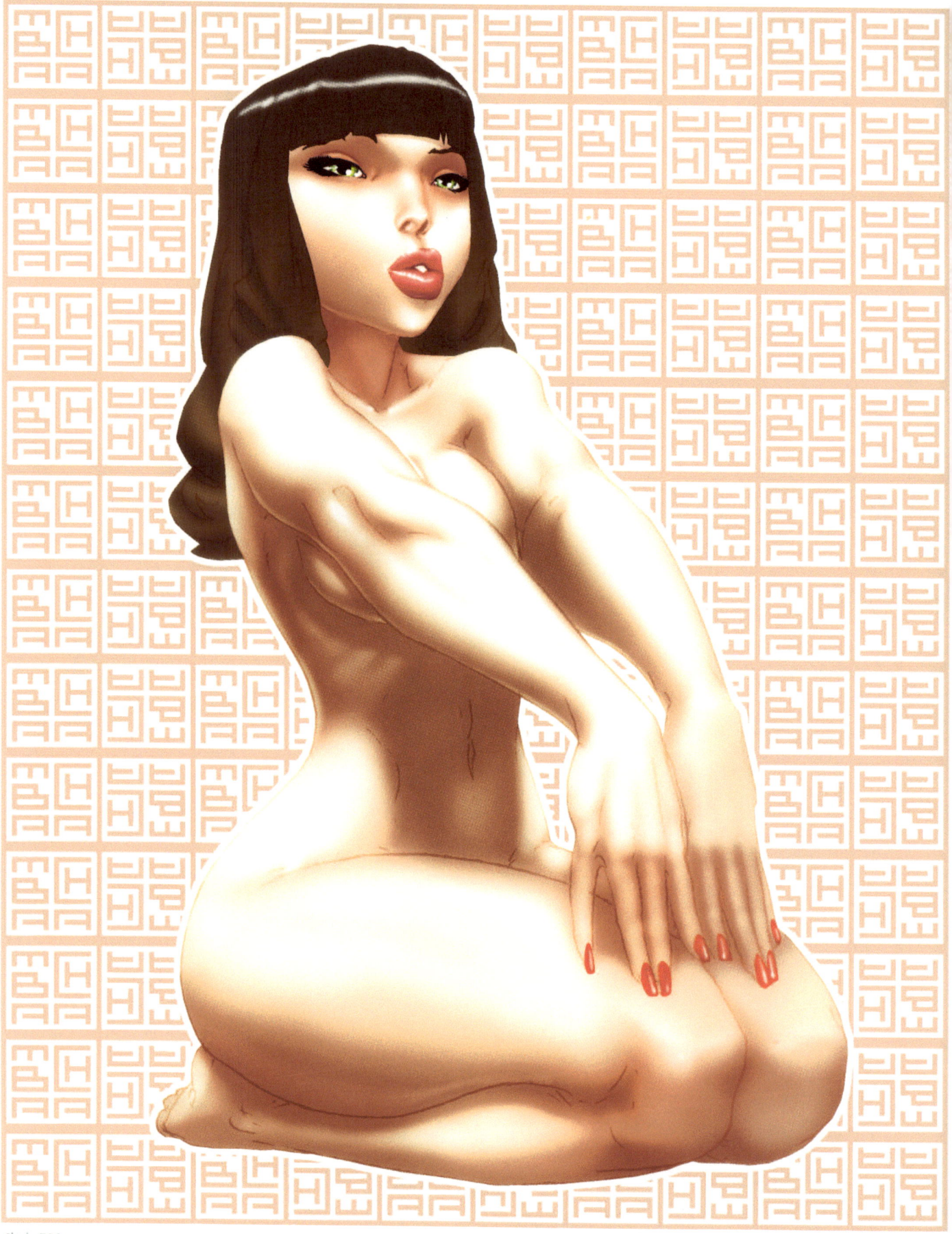

ChickaTOO

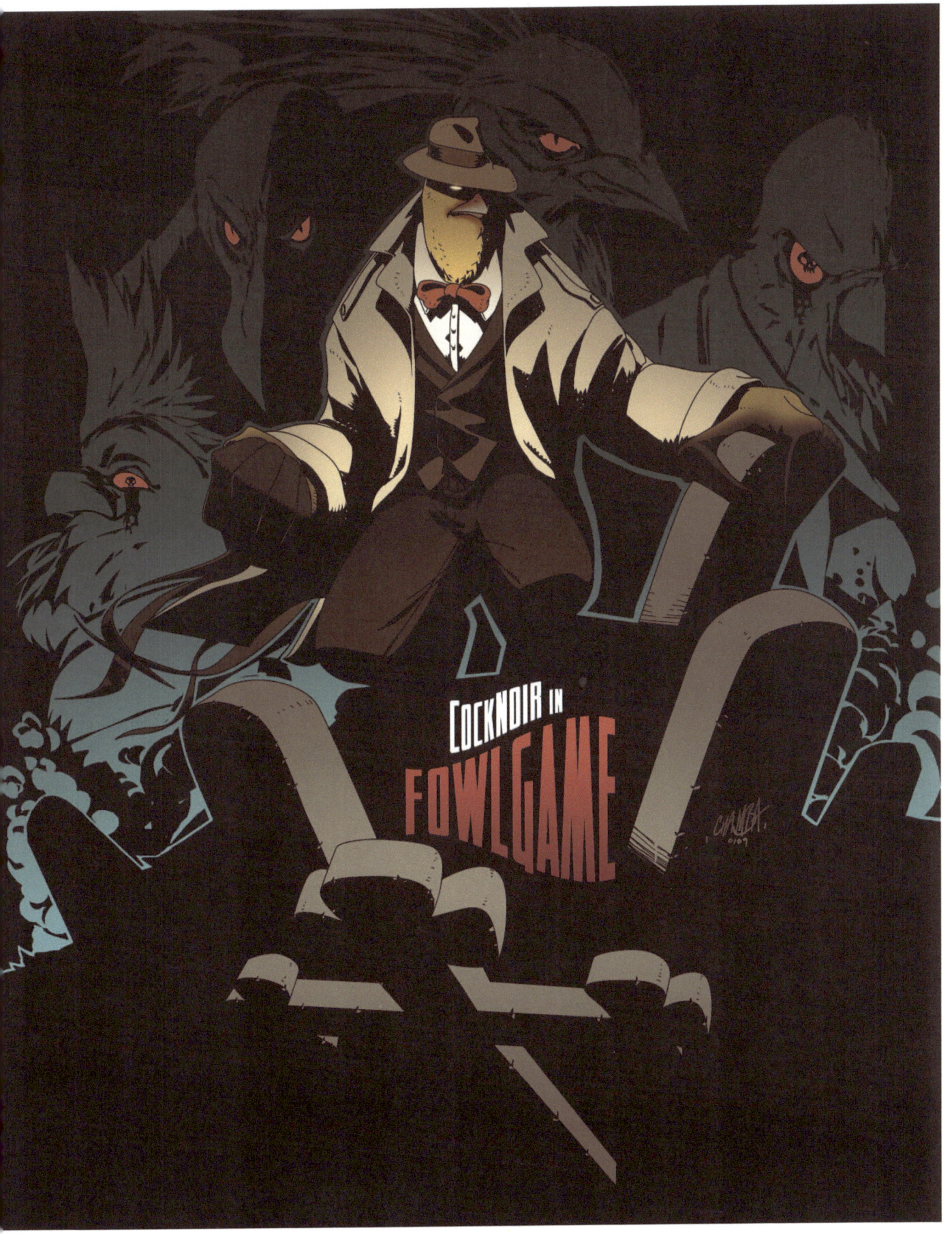

COCKNOIR IN

FOWL GAME

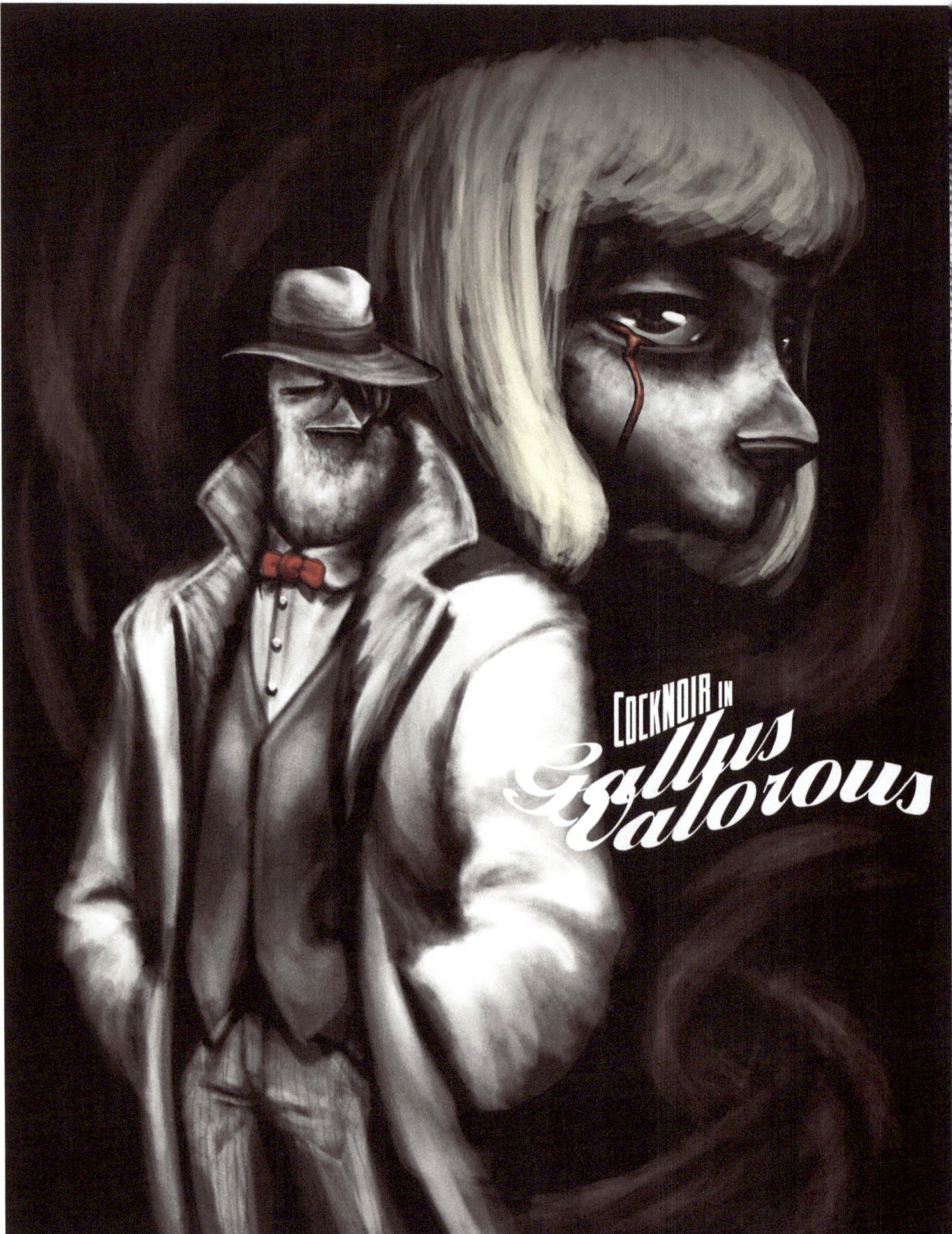

COCKNOIR IN *Gallus Valorous*

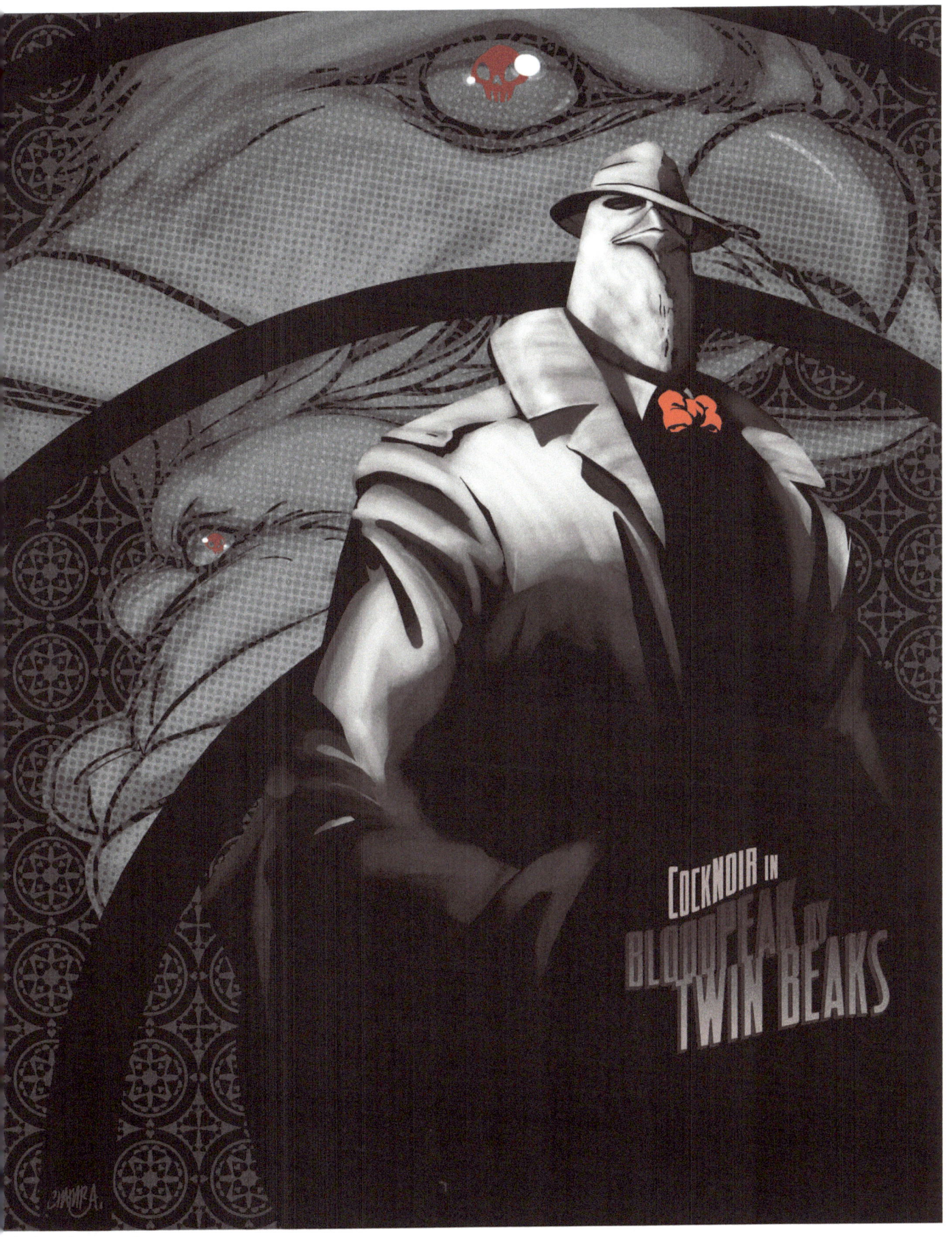

COCKNOIR in BLOODPEAK of TWIN BEAKS

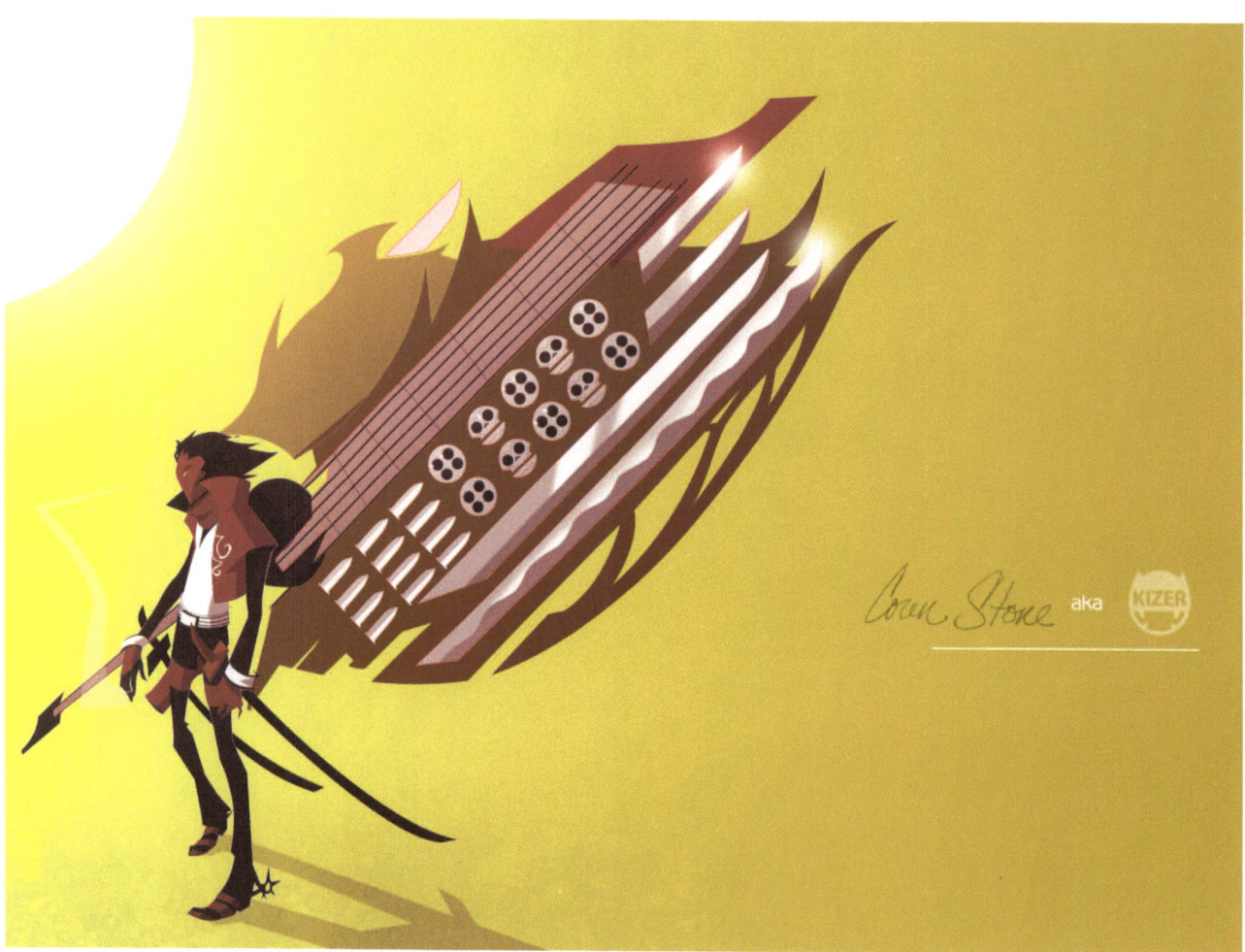

coranSTONE *aka* KIZER

"I guess I officially got started in the digital arts world drawing weird faces, demons and superheroes with MS paint back when I was in junior high", says Coran, whose fellow students were somewhat surprised that the could create highly detailed pieces using just a low tech program and a mouse.

After graduating from high school and studying graphic design, Coran stumbled across a couple of artists and began coloring their line work in Photoshop. "While watching them I was pretty astounded," he recalls. "I had originally thought that Photoshop was mainly used for specific purposes like flyers, posters and business cards."

After realizing Photoshop's potential, "I totally decided to give it a go". But, surprisingly, Coran didn't pick up where he'd left off with MS Paint. "I started by creating the cosmos. Yup, I started with planets, stars, supernovas, nebulae and so on. I guess I felt that if I could create these things in Photoshop then anything after that was possible".

Contact: web www.kizer180.deviantart.com   e-mail kizer180@yahoo.com

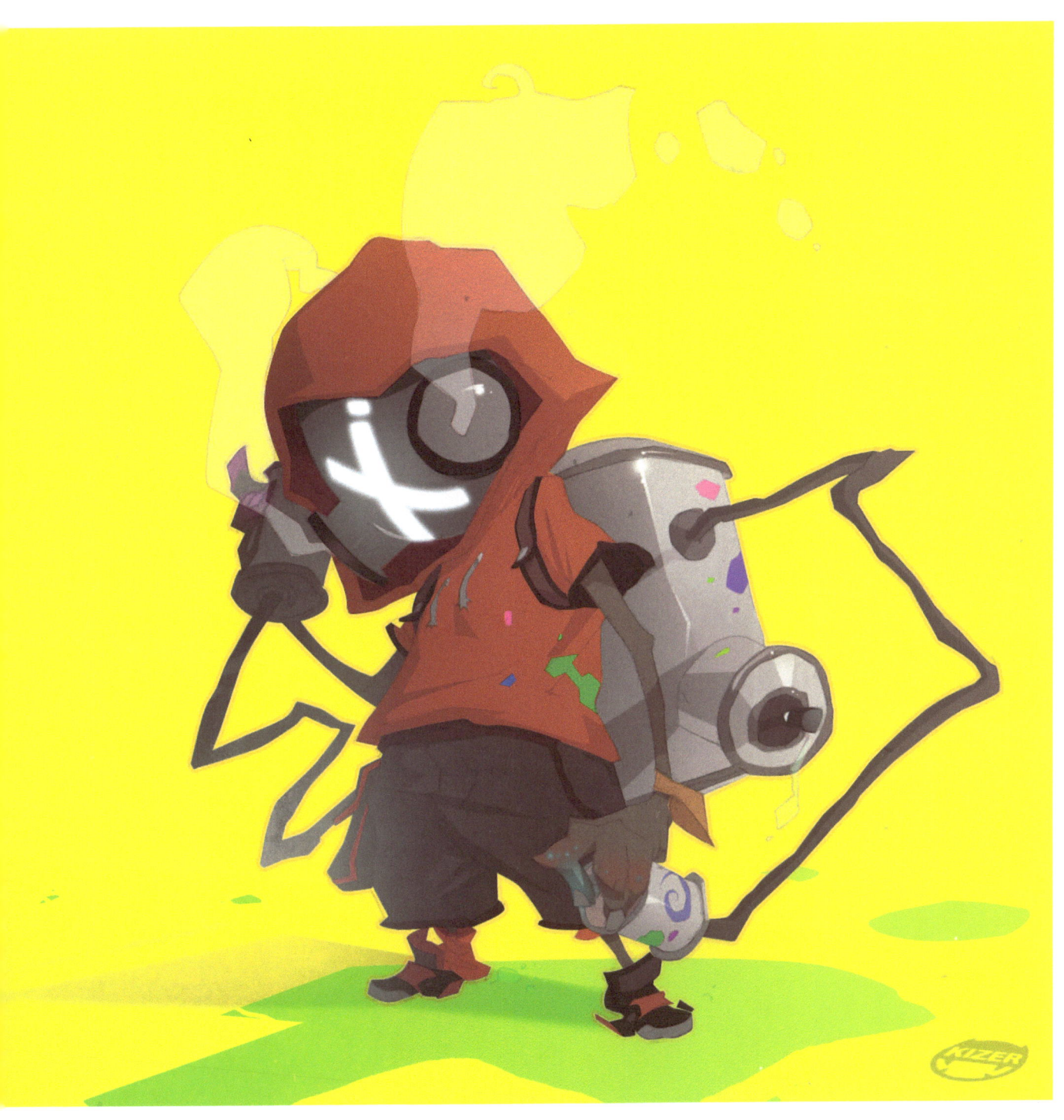

hiti

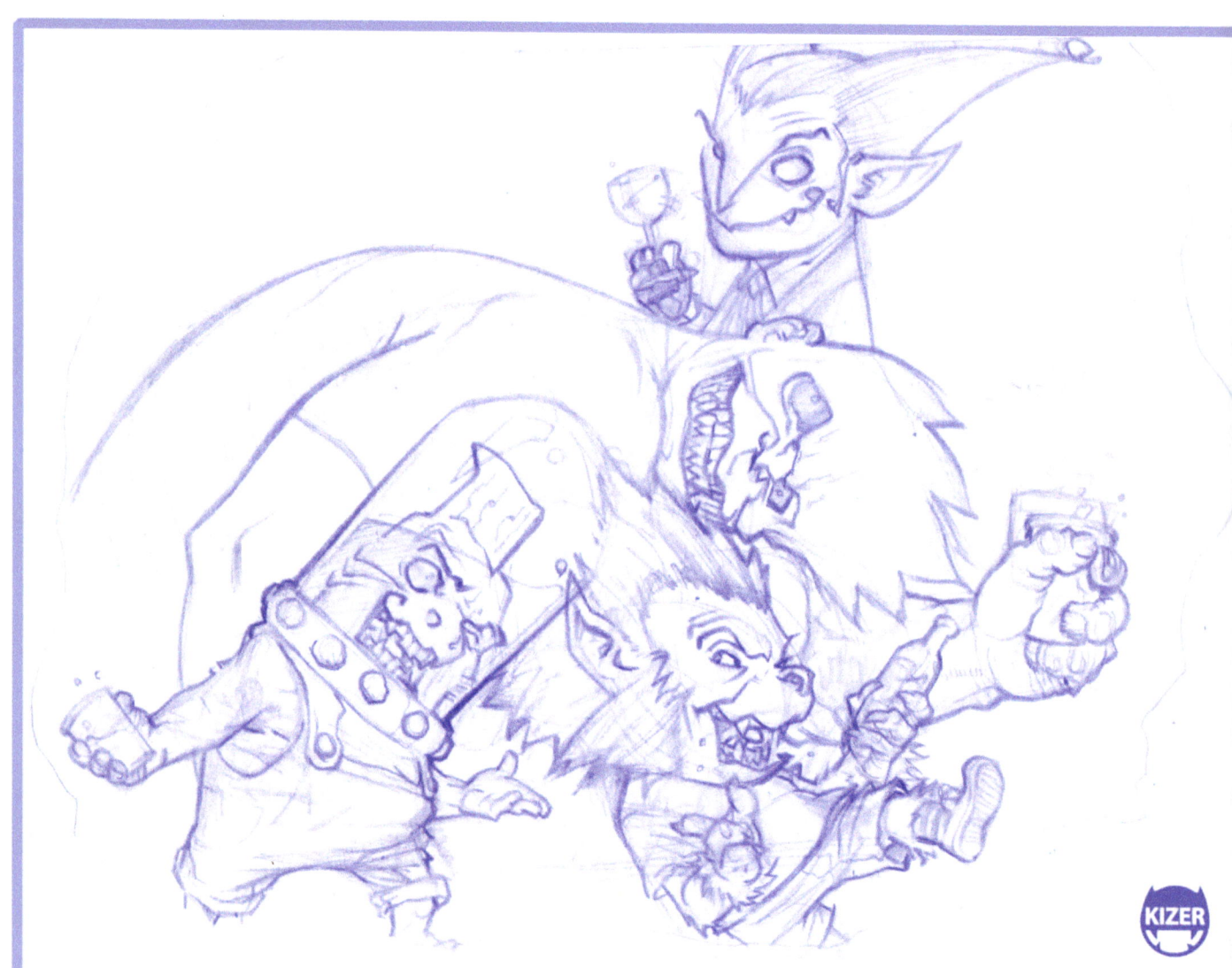

Cryptics

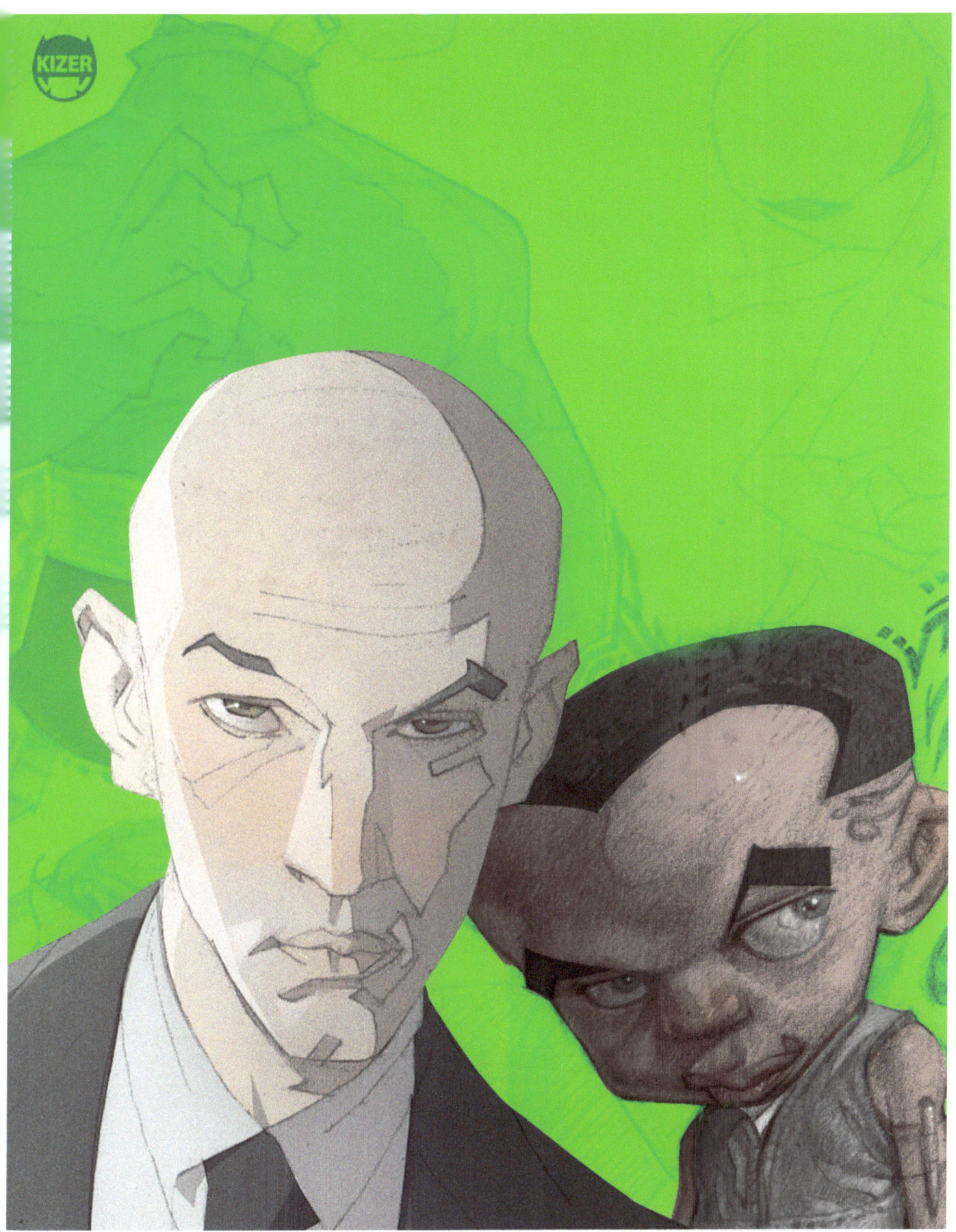

KIZER

Professor and Lil'Blade

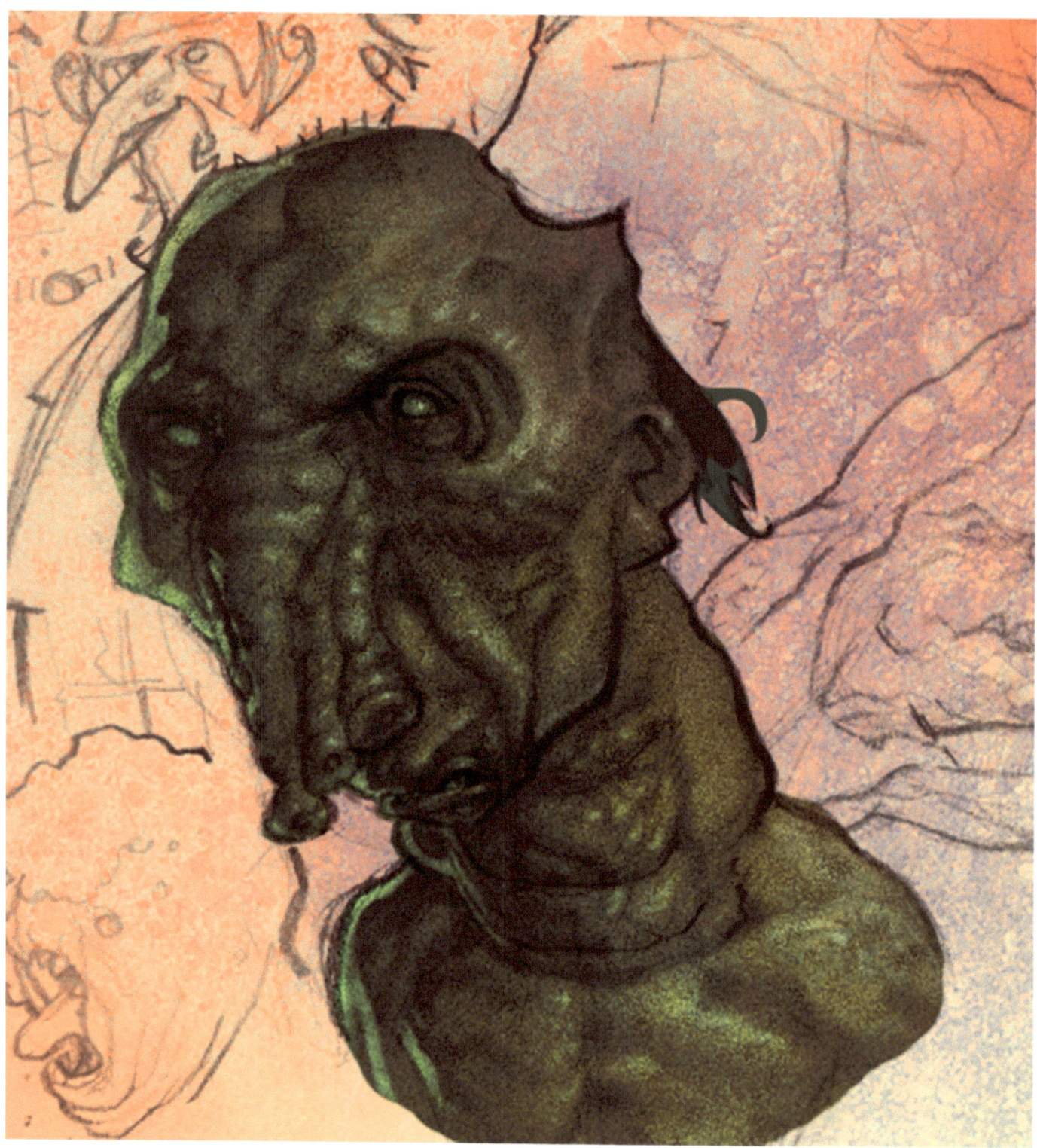

Alien Practice

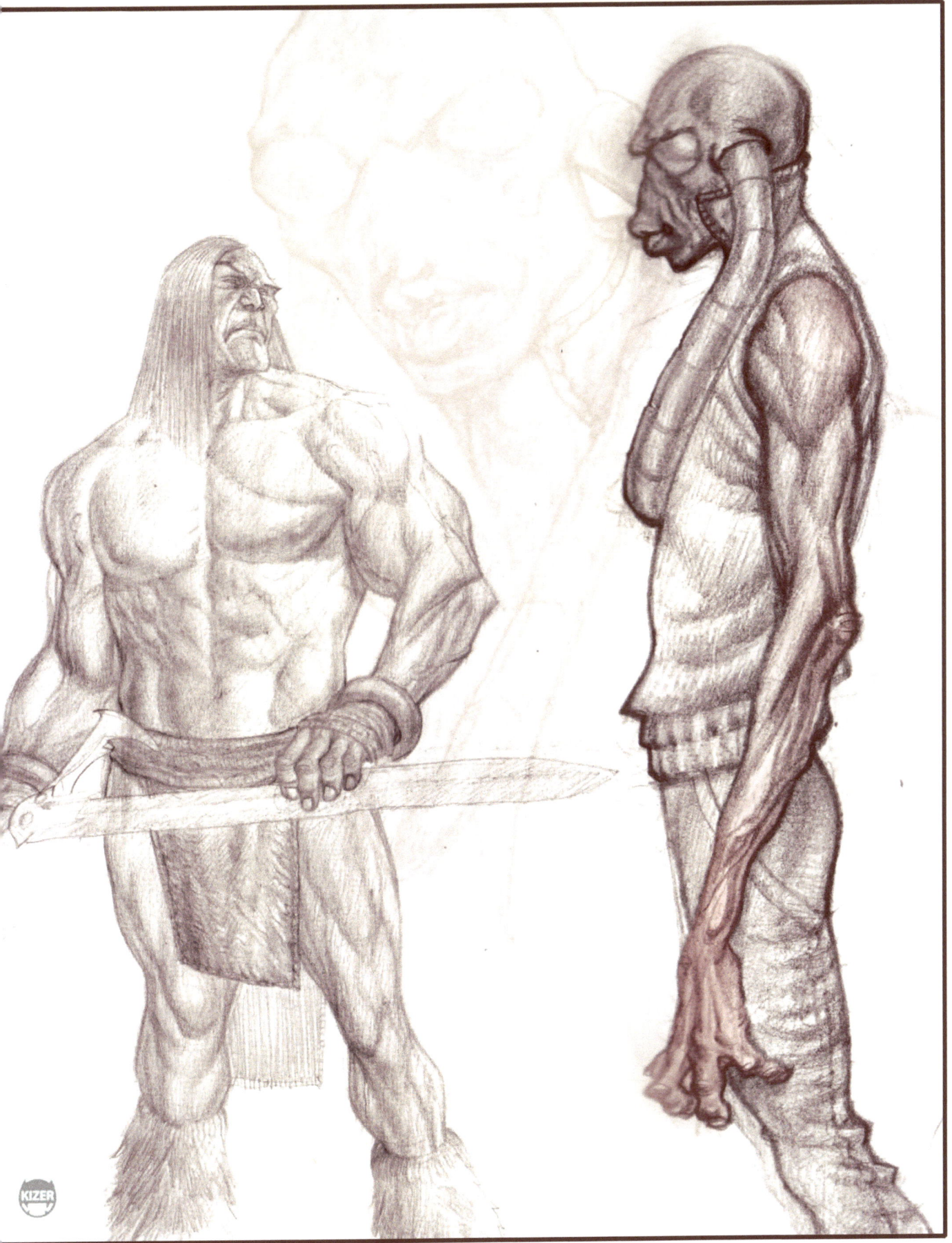

Warrior and Alien

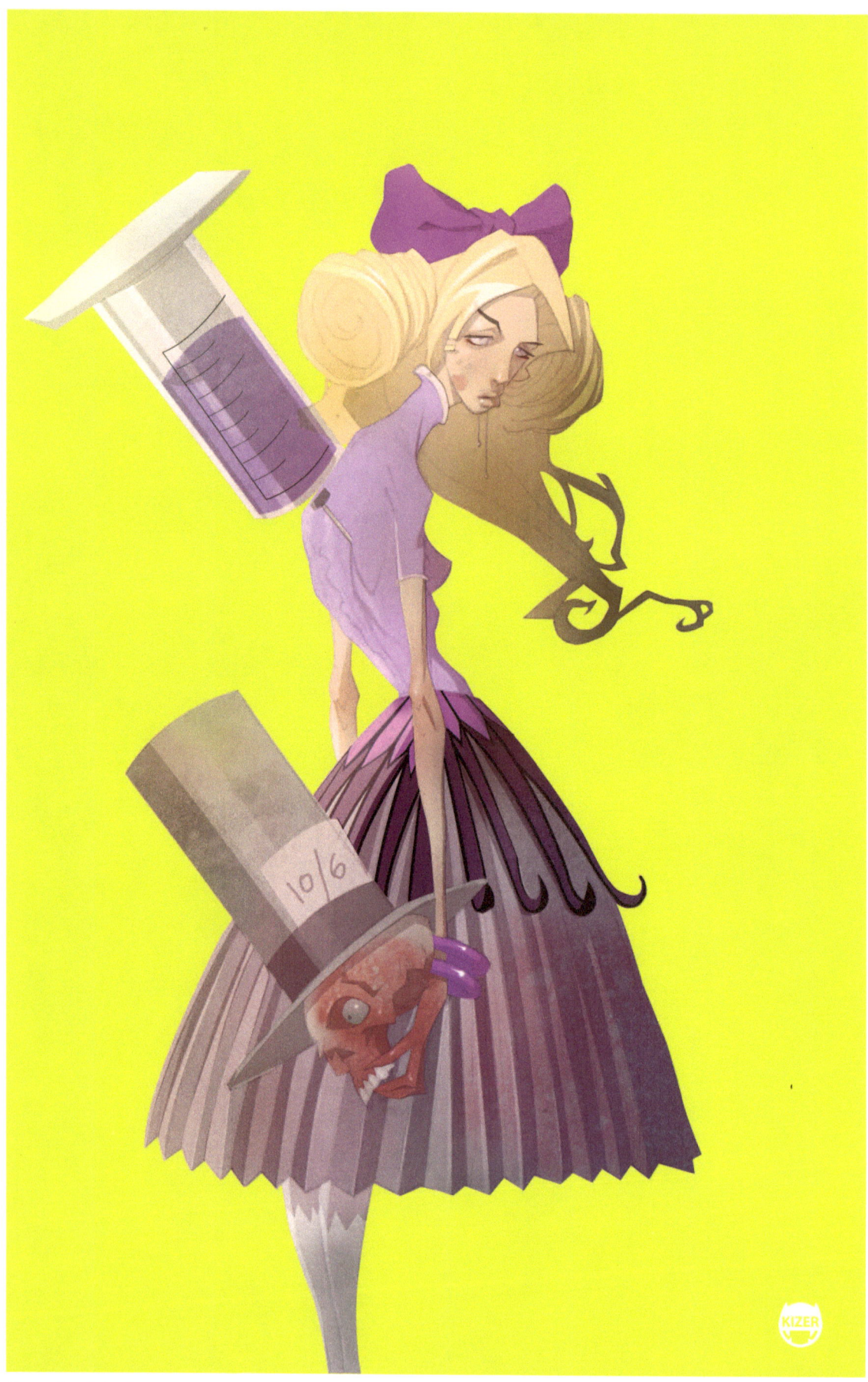

Alice in Wonderland

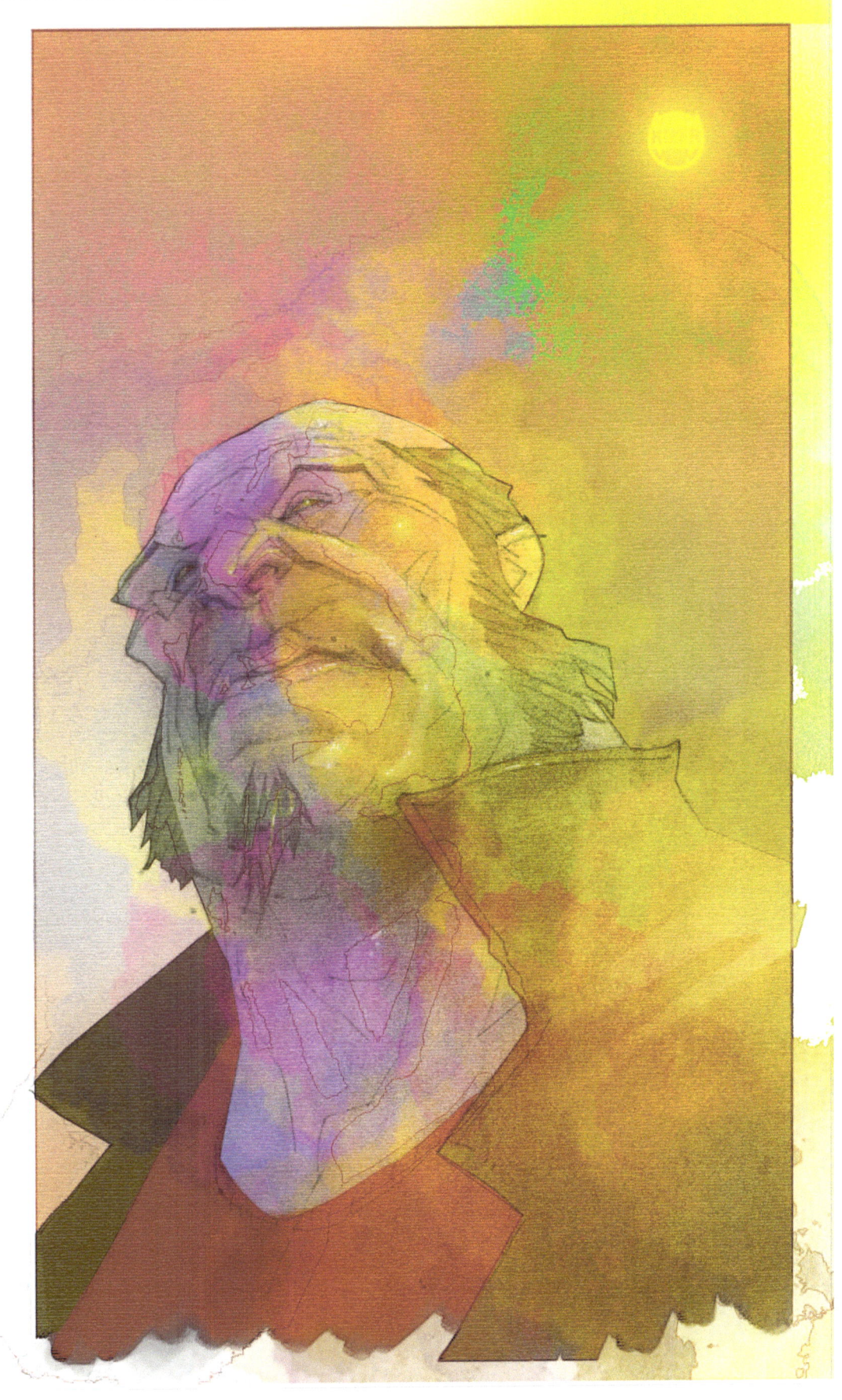

Distured Thoughts

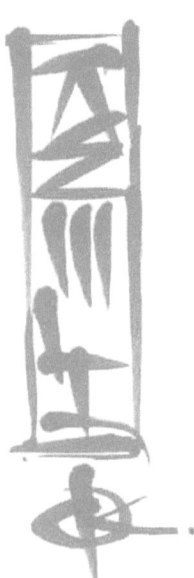

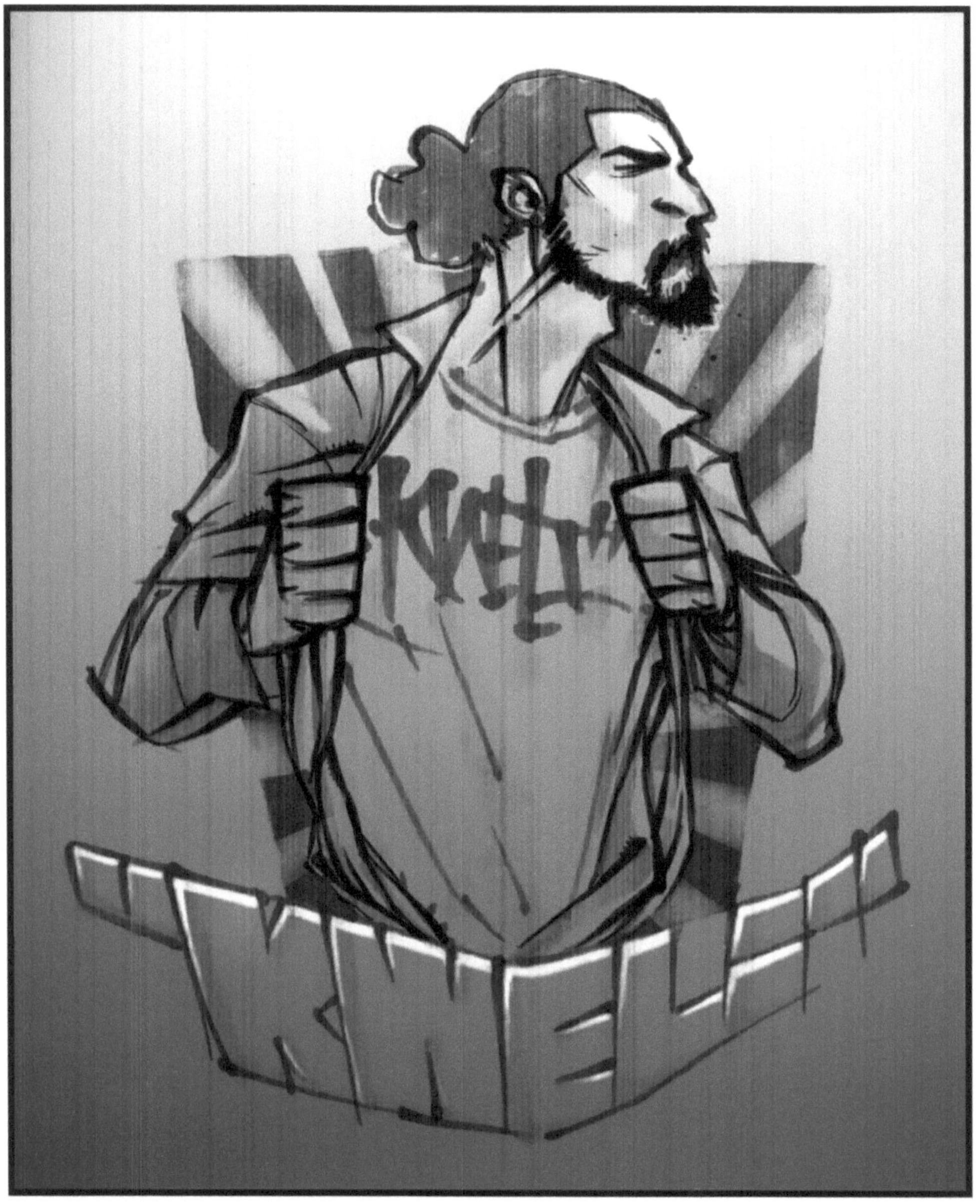

christopherCOPELAND *aka* Kweli

Chris "KWELI" Copeland was born and raised in the inner-city of Chicago where he took advantage of the surrounding culture that would influence his art. In the beginning of his art journey, along with his 2 brothers and the use of crayons and whatever he could find to write on, any surface would come to life in the form of graffiti.

After being chased by local law-enforcement one too many times, he decided to move on with his work and combine it with an art form that would speak to more of a diverse crowd... comics and animation.

Now he spends his time creating work for the people in the comics and animation industry while still GETTING UP and MAKING HIS MARK in the minds of people from all over...and now YOU!"

Contact: web www.ianspirational.blogspot.com   e-mail chali2naj5@gmail.com

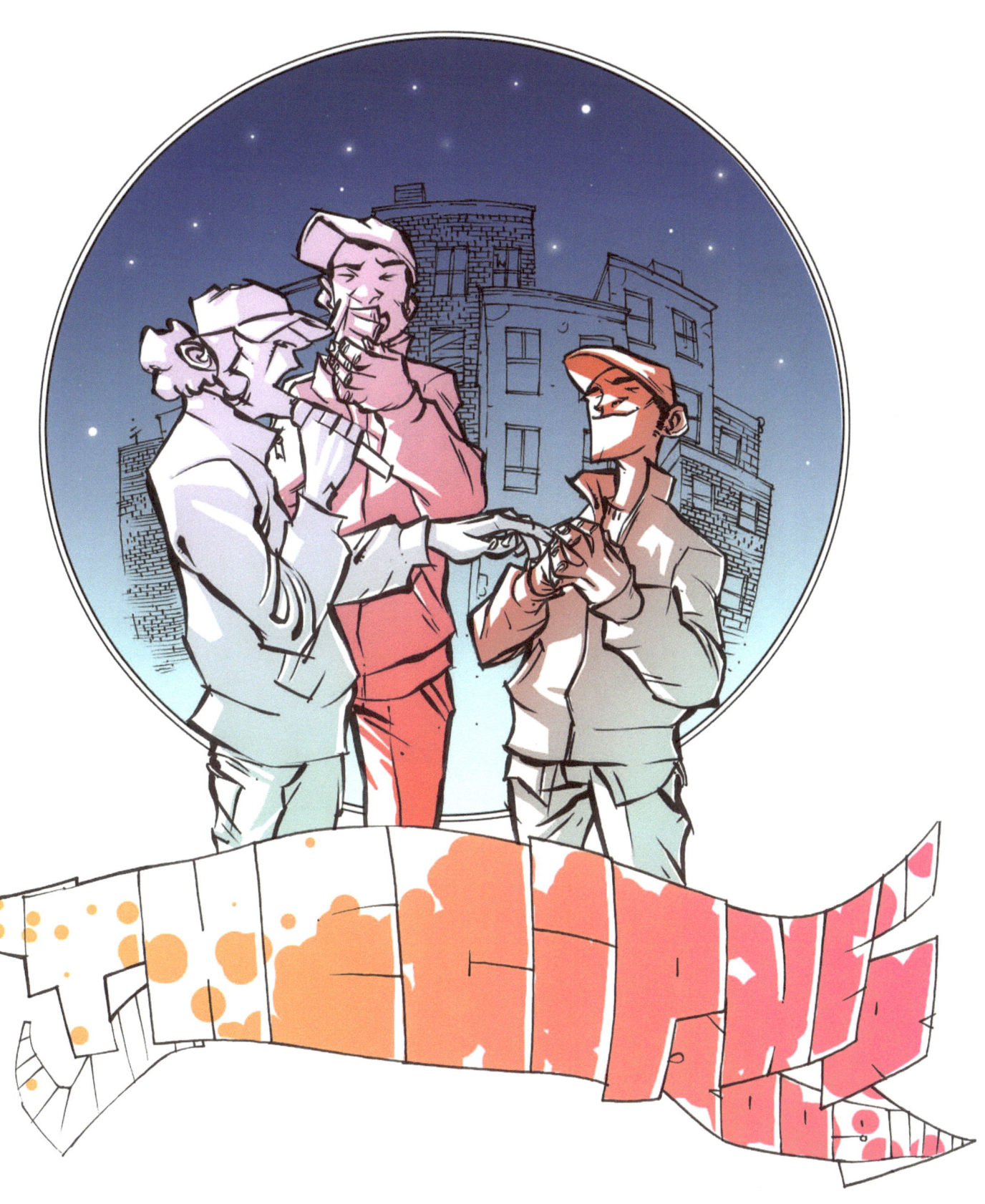

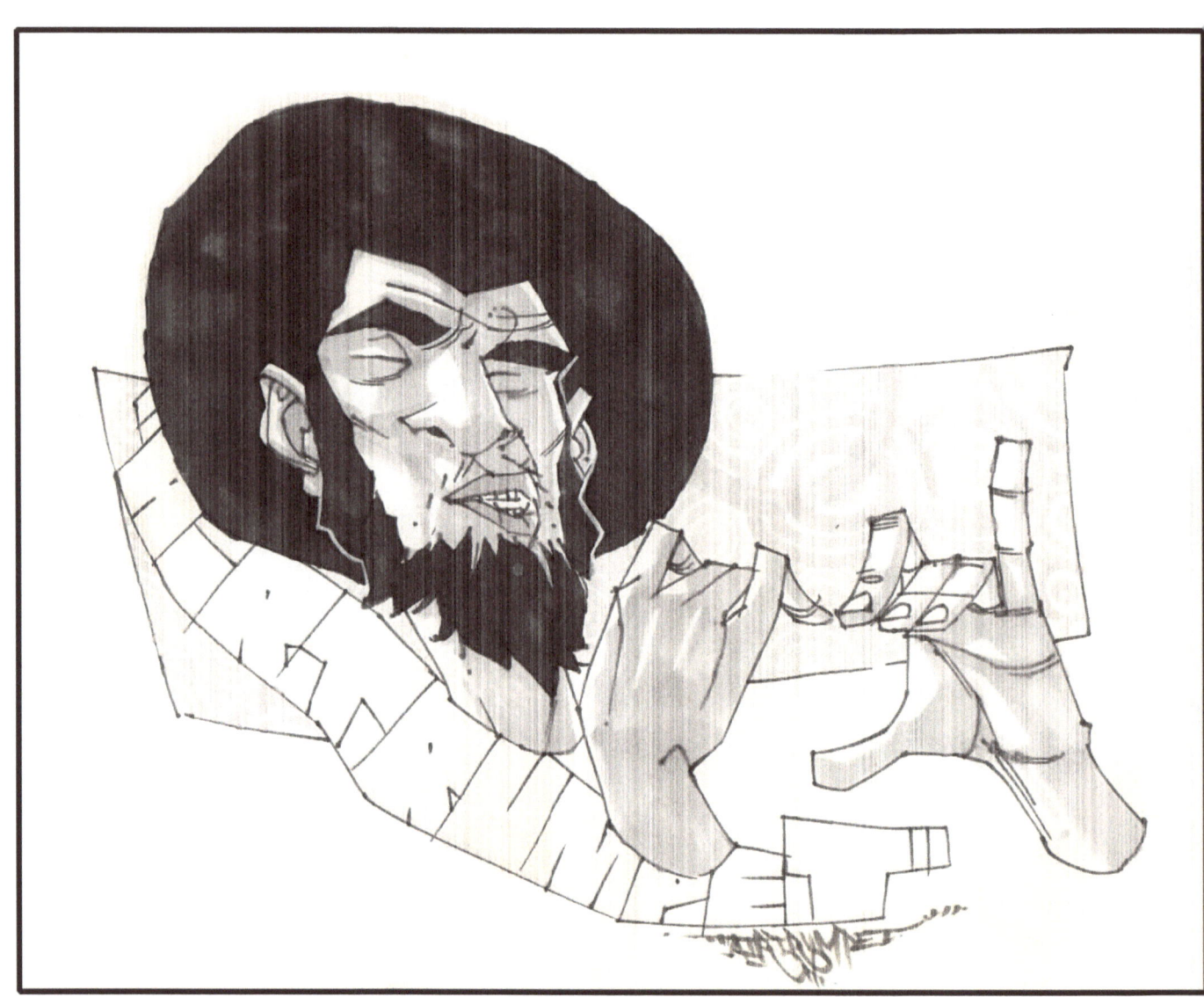

Air Trumpet

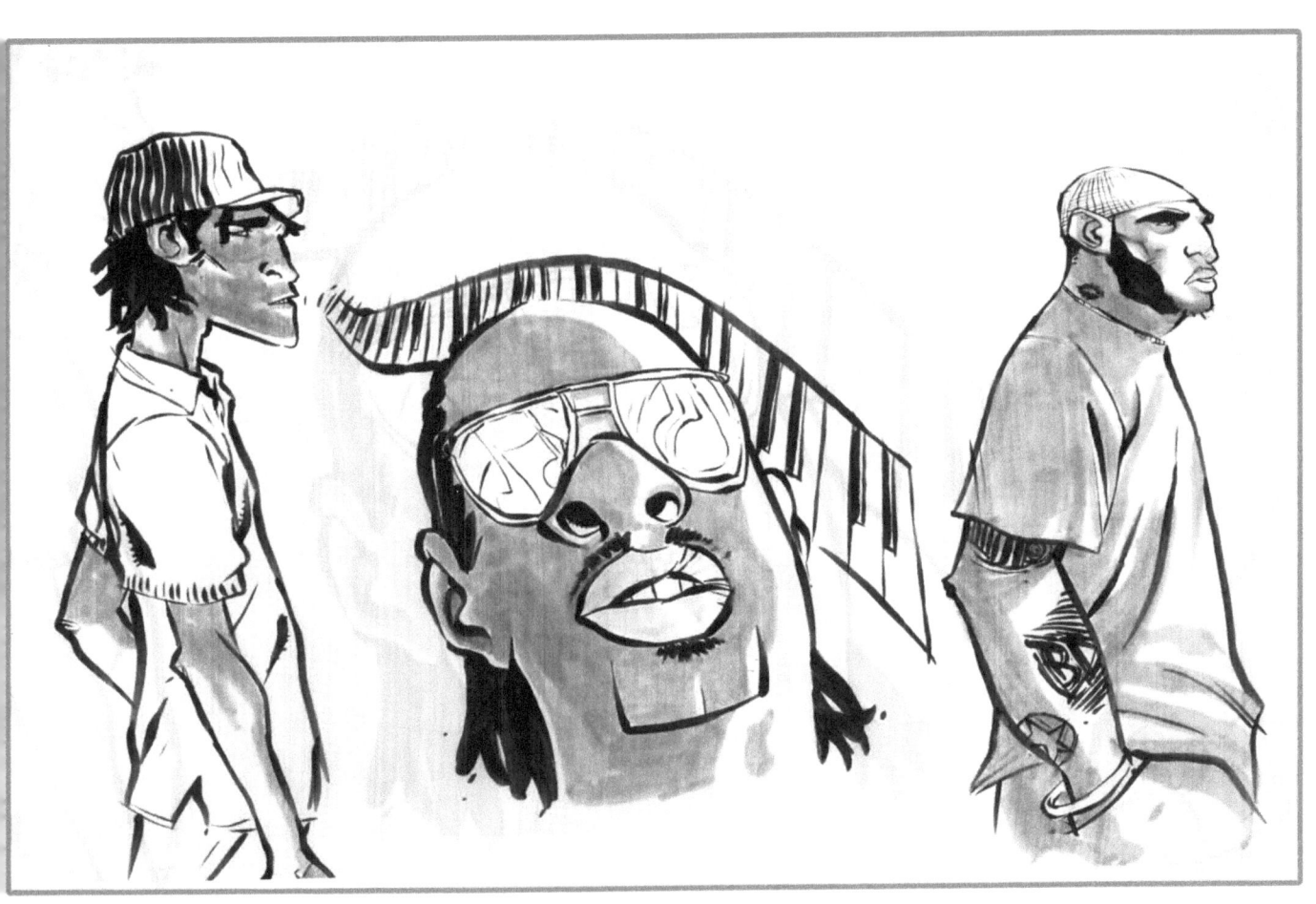

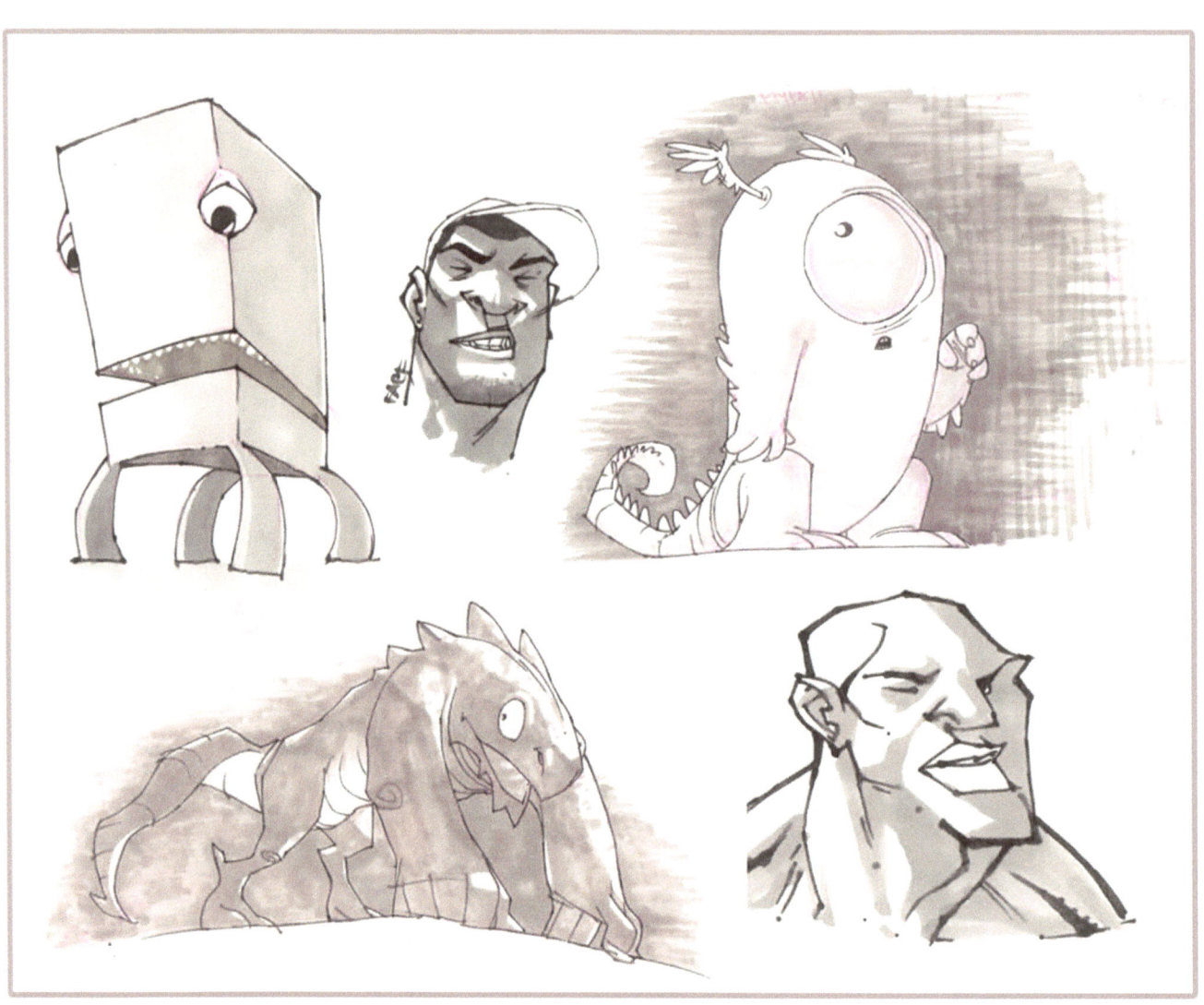

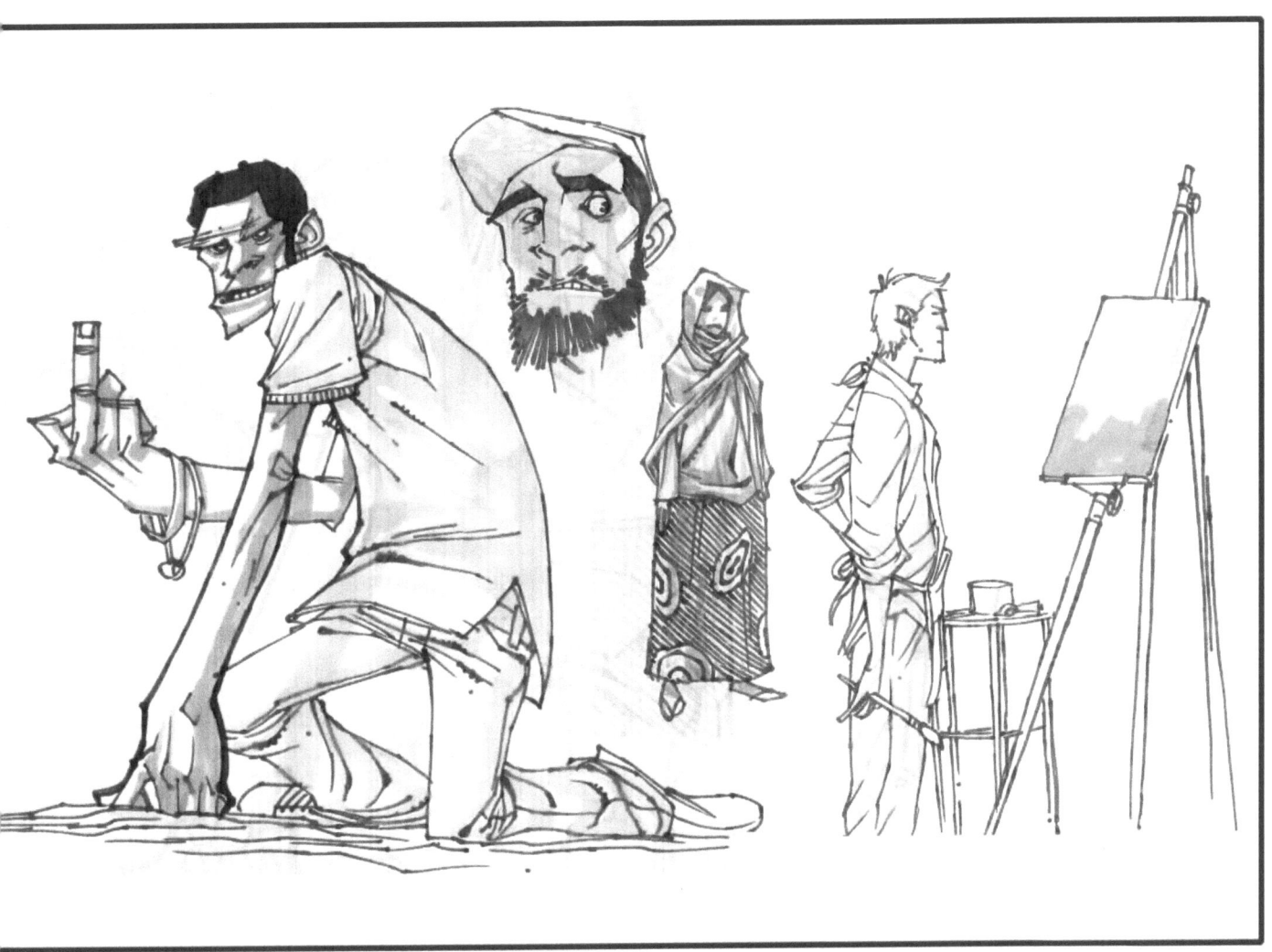

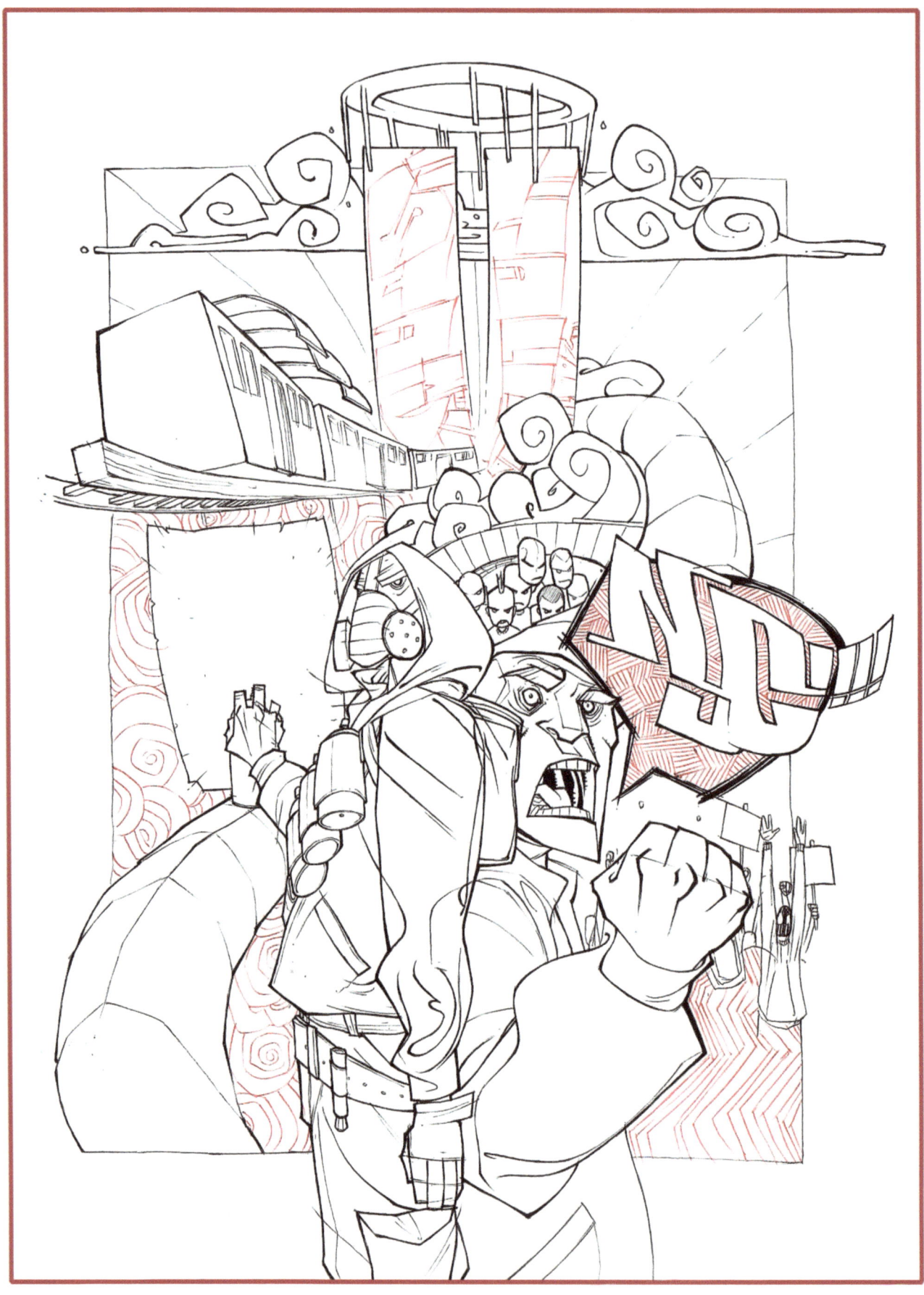

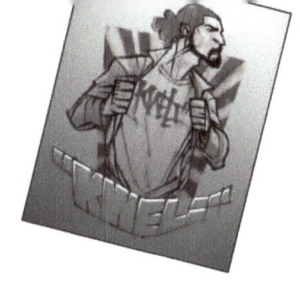

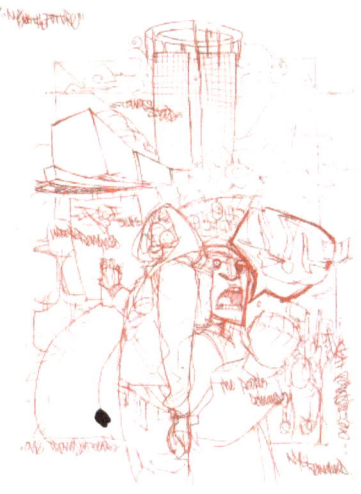

Step 1 is establishing the flow of the piece, kinda playing with the different elements, and seeing how far I can push, or how much stuff can I put in there without the image becoming cluttered with STUFF.

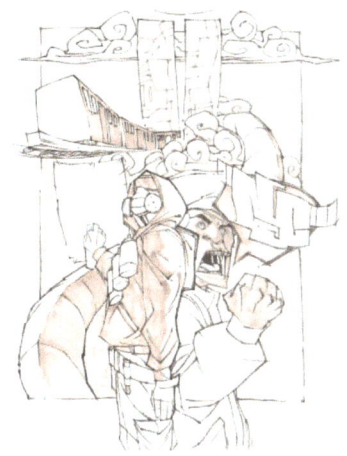

Step 2 is the tryout stage, this one is my favorite stage. I love playing with the gray markers, (as you can see with my sketches) so this is a fun part for me to kinda see where I want to go with the lighting, and also to play with the final composition a little bit. Also what helps with the markers is the finality of the line, they are really simple, and demand your attention. Fun stuff.

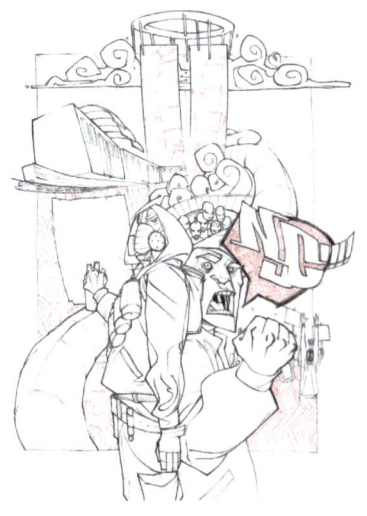

Step 3 this is the final stage, and the more tedious part, I ink with a PaperMate ball point pen sometimes, and this is the part where I have to fight my A.D.D. and really get the best out of my lines so that the coloring part is more precise, and easy...

Step 4...colors...where are they....oh...well......CHECK OUT VOLUME 2, SOON!

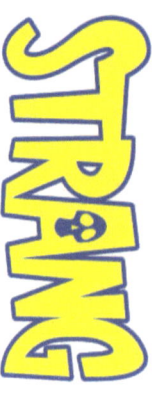

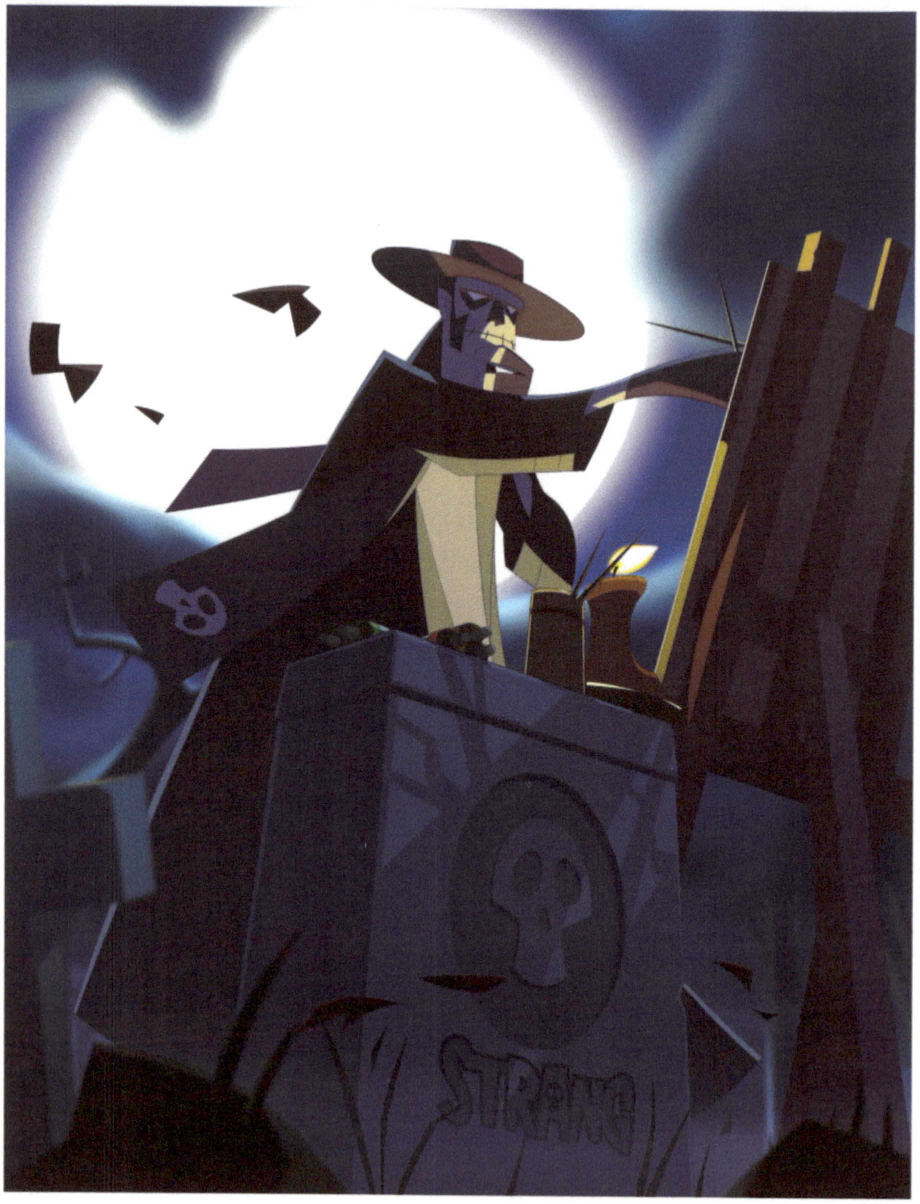

bobSTRANG *aka* Von Toten

Bob Strang was born and raised in Jersey. Thoroughly influenced by B-Horror Movies and 1950's style and music, Bob uses that passion in his illustrations.

Contact: web www.vontoten.deviantart.com   e-mail vontoten@comcast.net

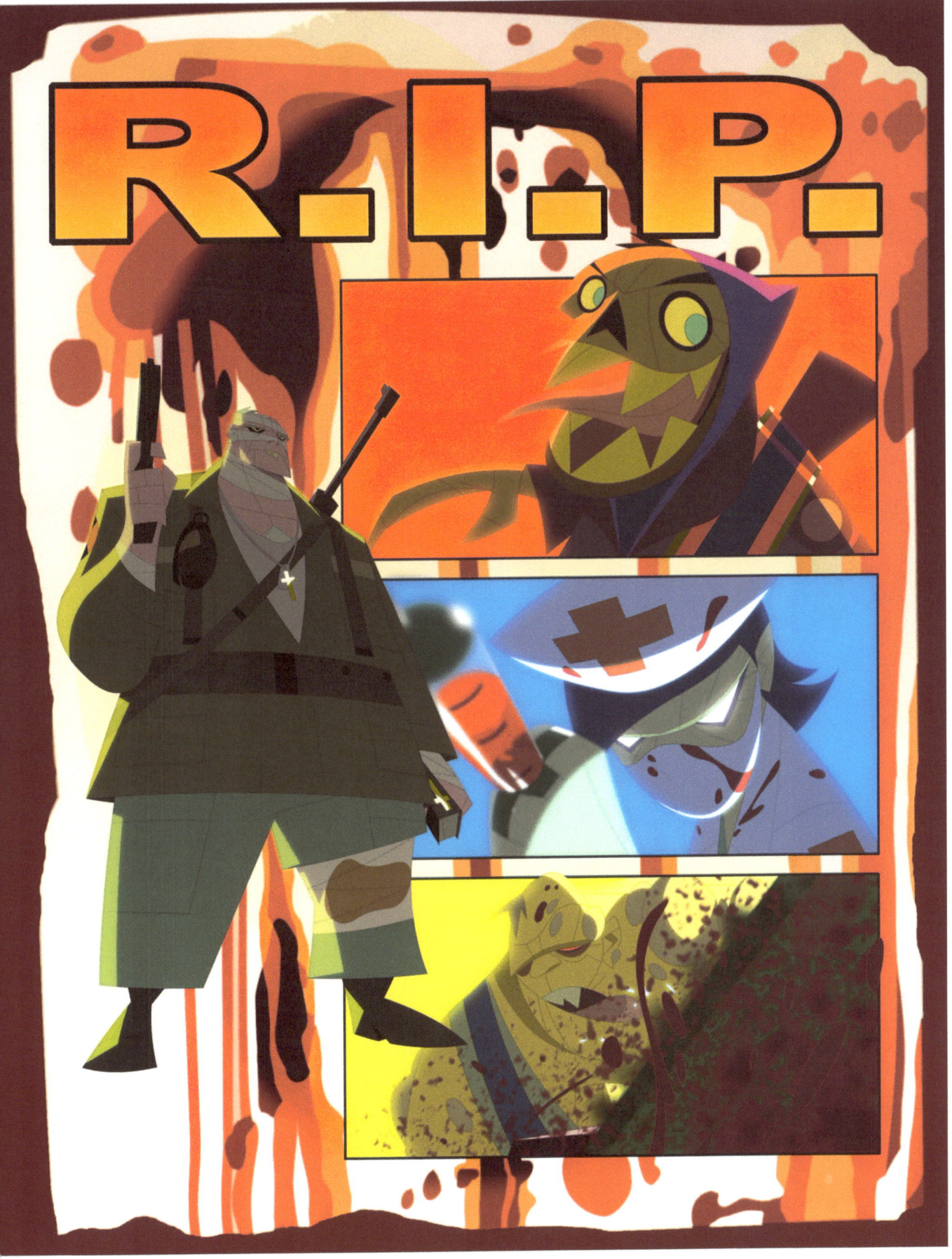

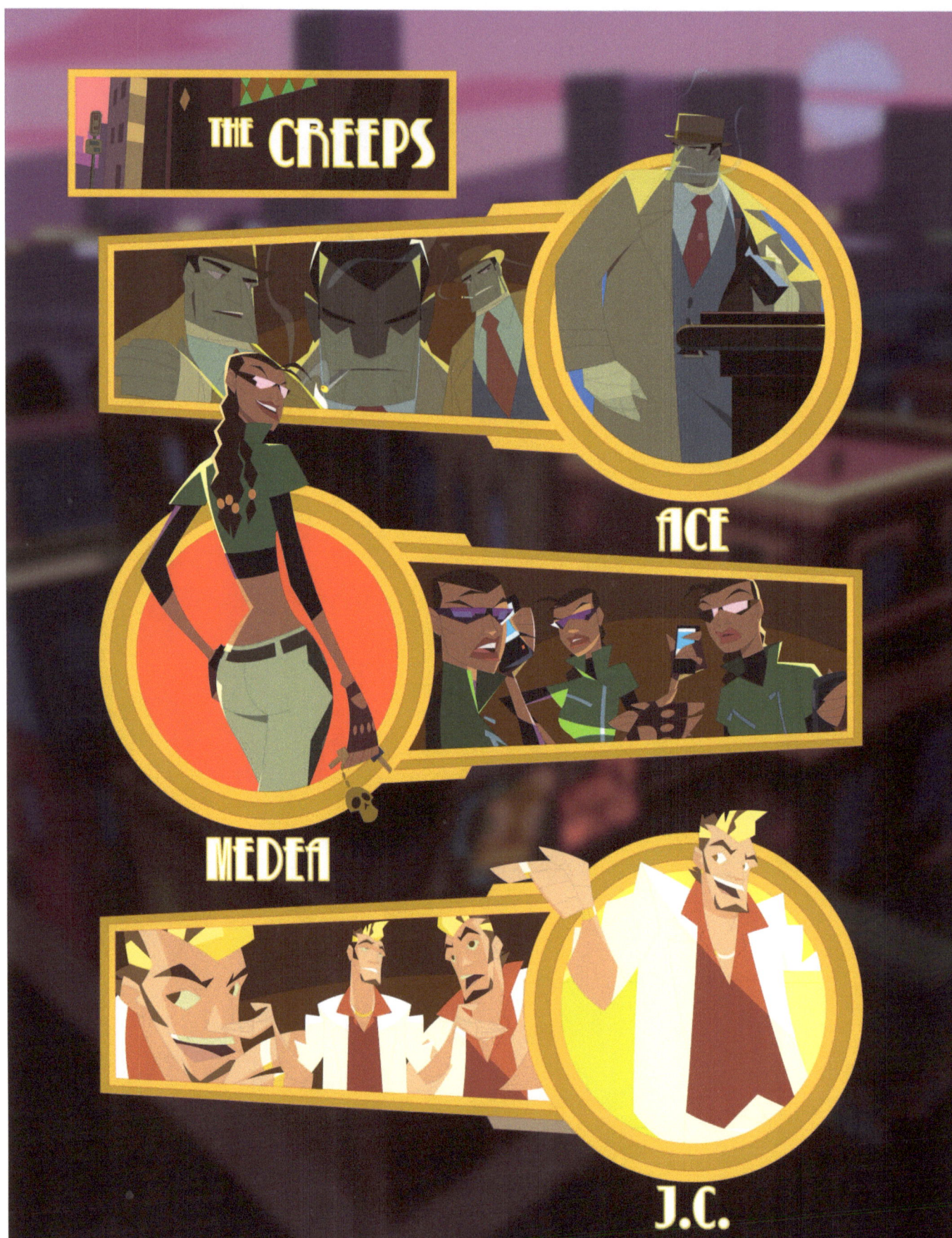

THE CREEPS

ACE

MEDEA

J.C.

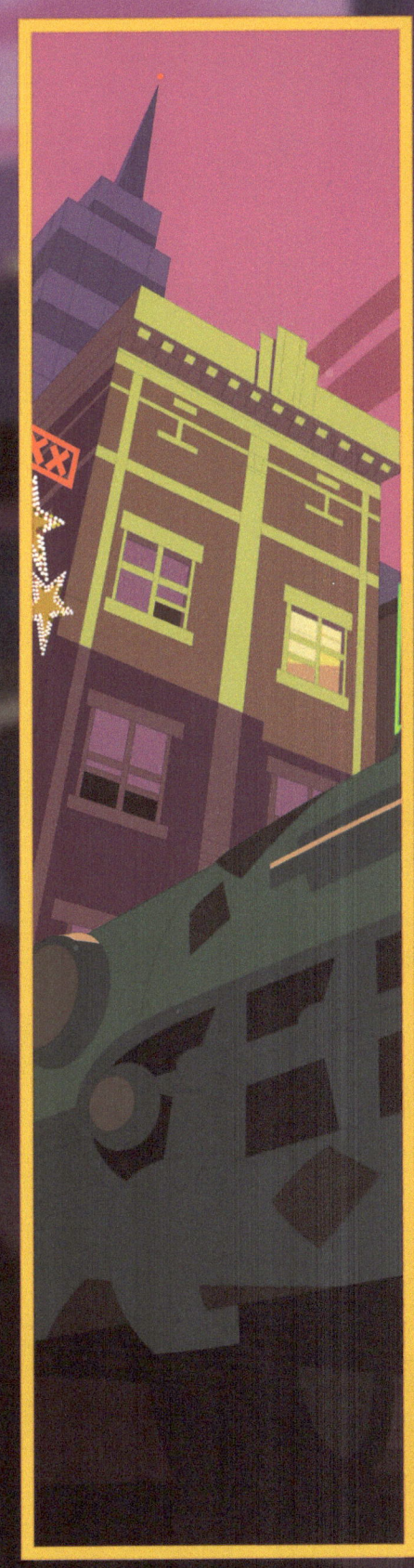

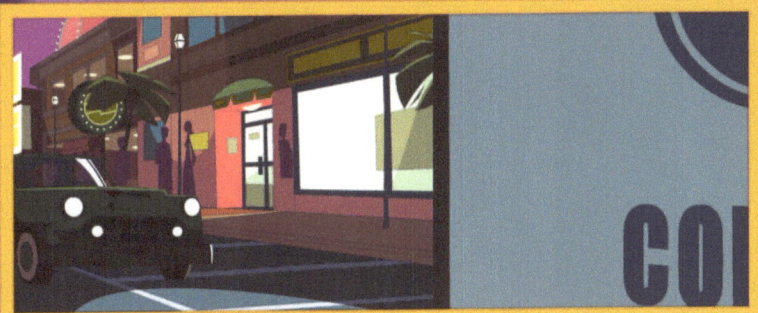

CO

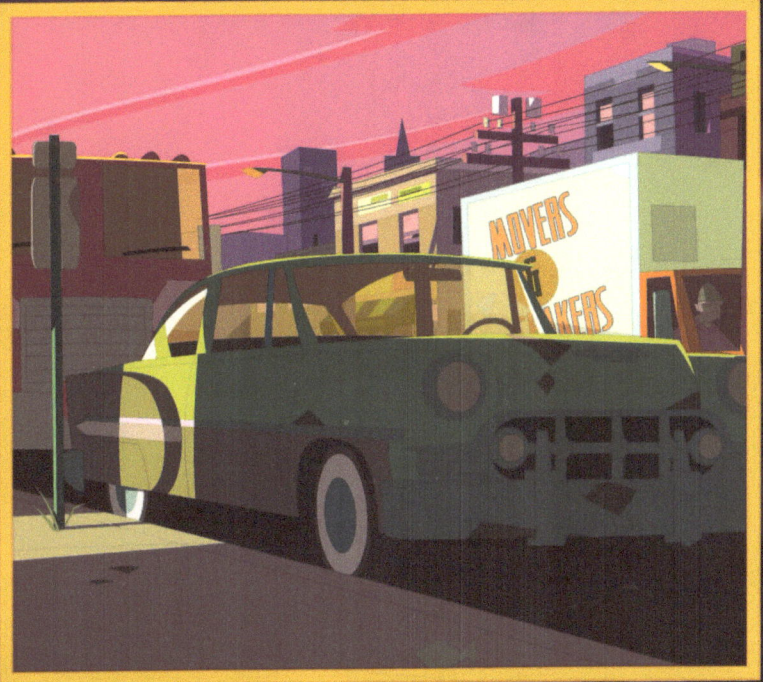

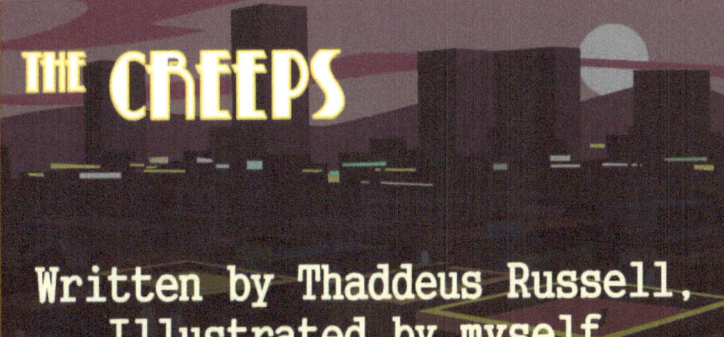

THE CREEPS

Written by Thaddeus Russell,
Illustrated by myself.
Coming soon from Ape
Entertainment.

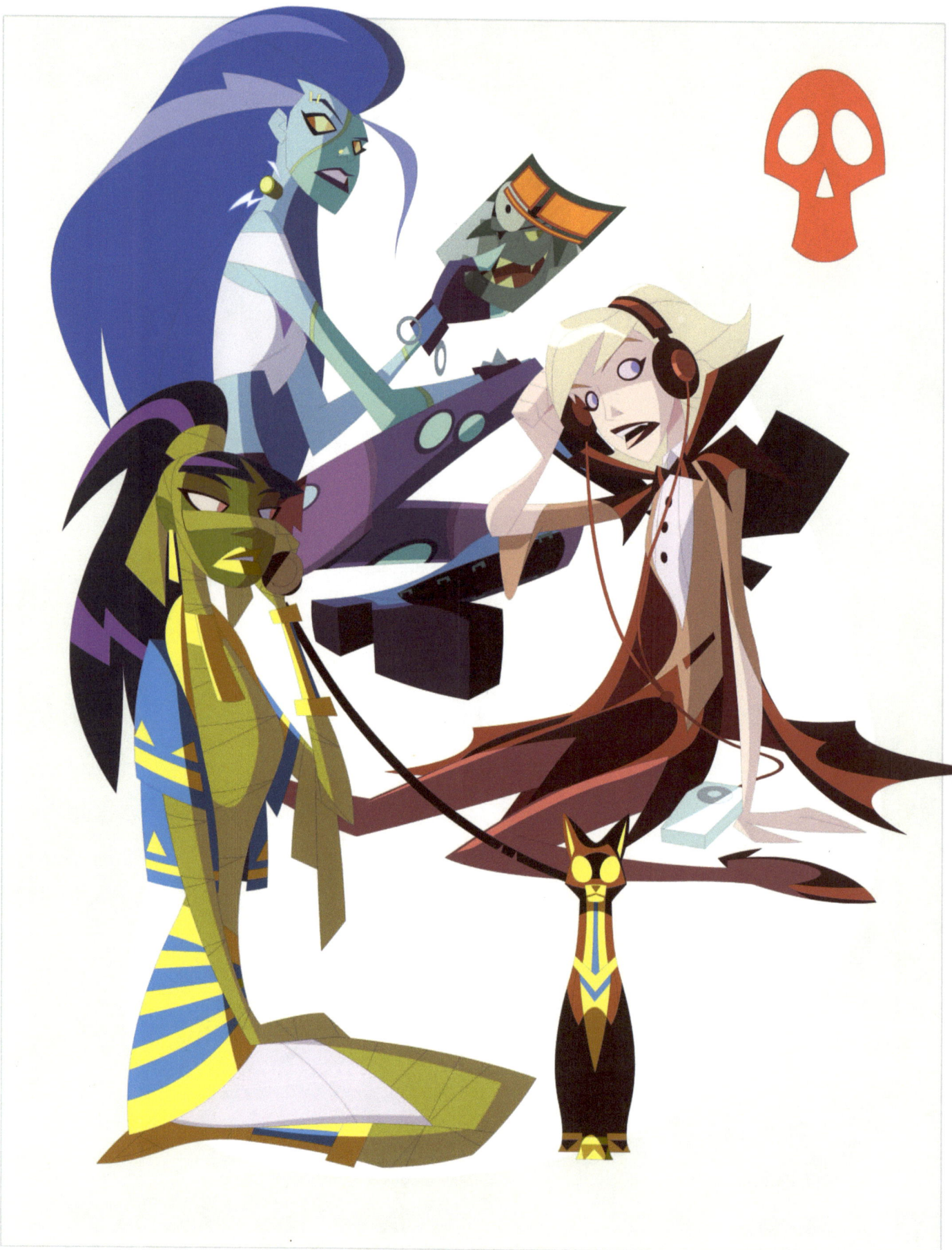

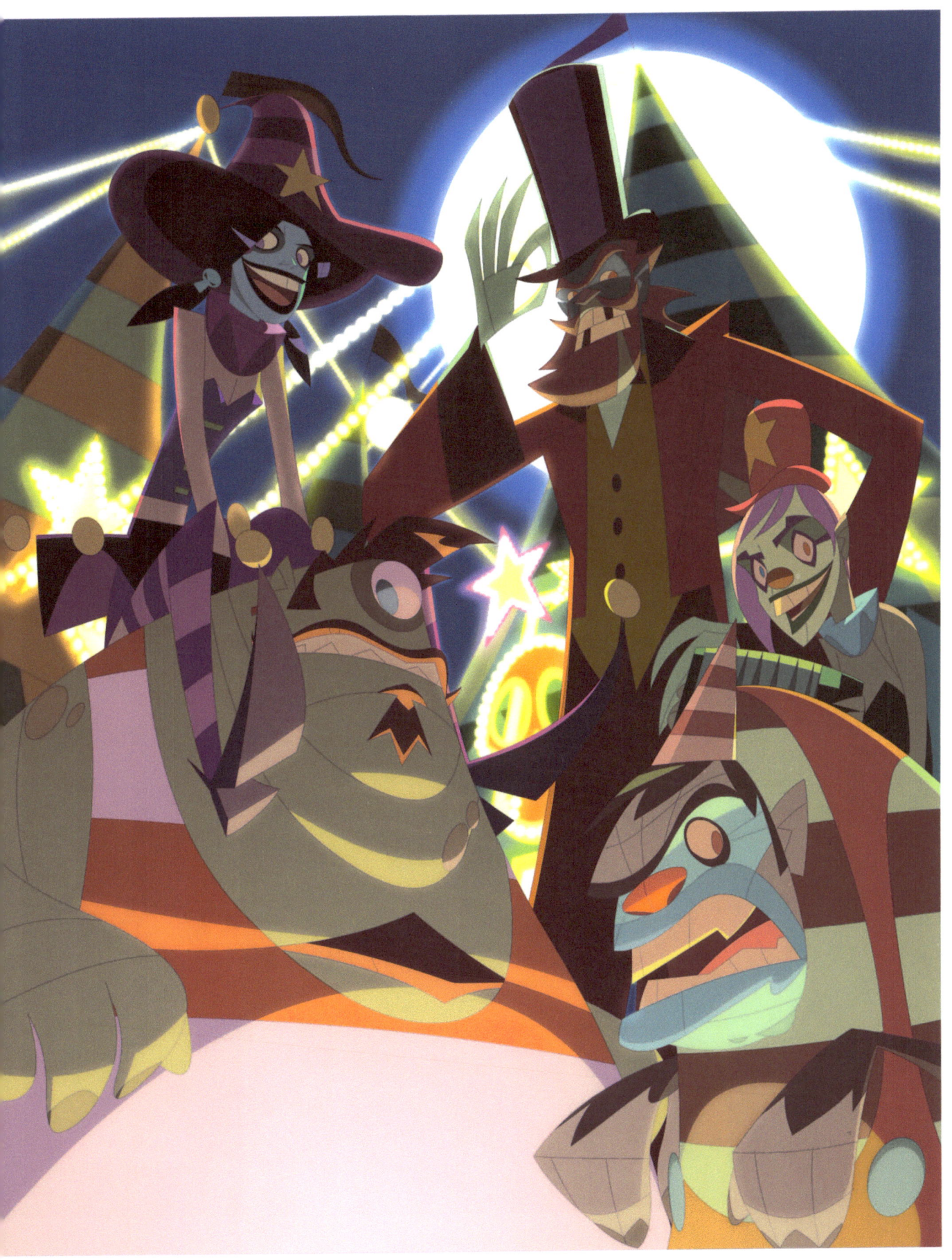

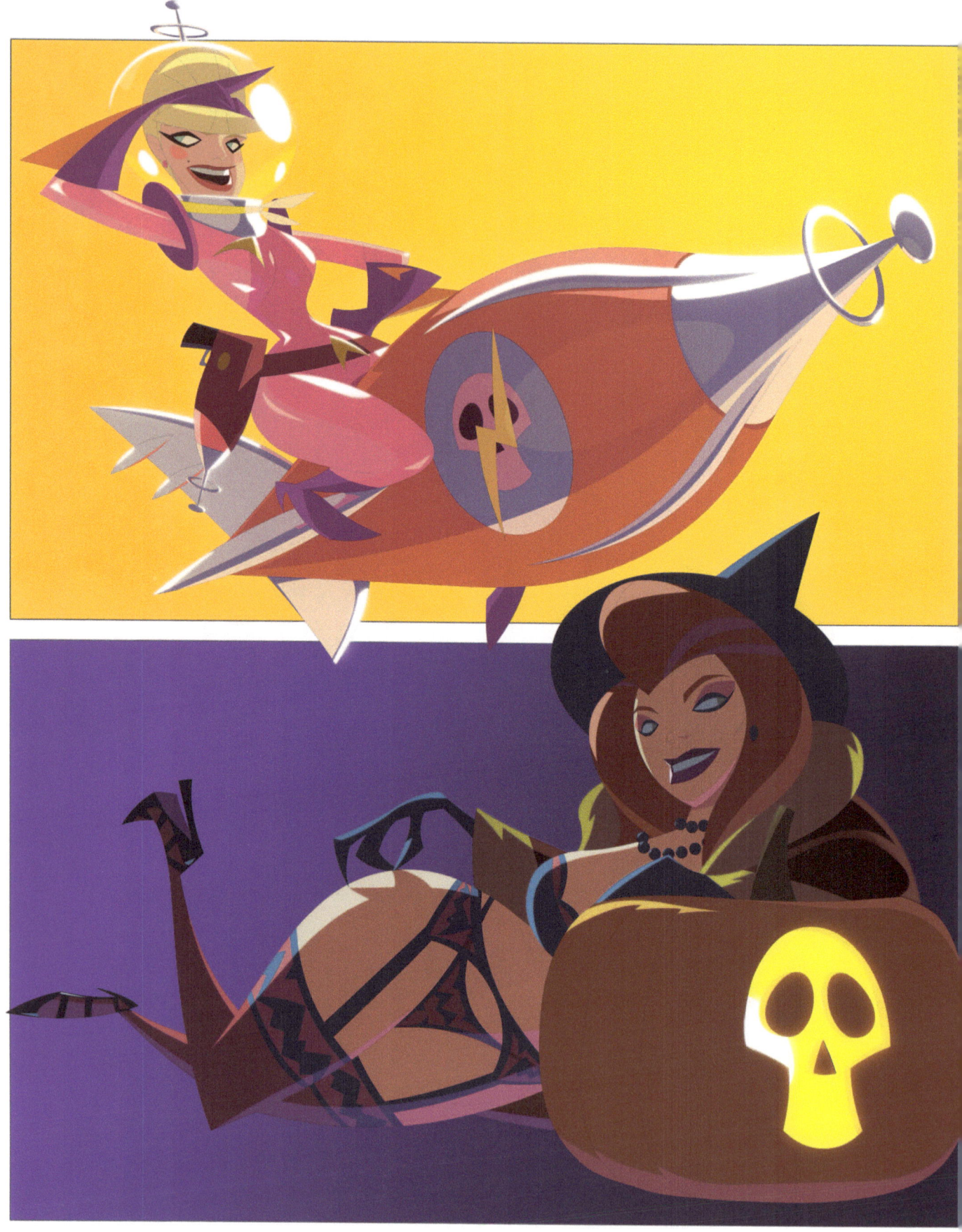

Rocket Girl and Witch

Top ten tips to getting your digital art printed and done right

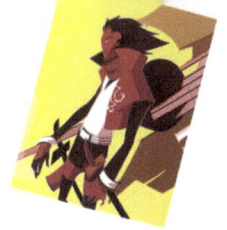

1. Make sure your file settings are correct. Simply have the file in CMYK format.

2. DPI and SIZE. Most printers want at least a 300 DPI file and working that DPI size at all times is best. If your final print is 8x10 then you should work that size or in that size ratio, never smaller. If you work in a smaller size and the printer has to enlarge your image then the final print might have a slight unwanted blur.

3. Font issues. One big waste of time in the printing business is not going into production because the artist did not include the fonts or did not turn the fonts into "art" or "rasterize" the fonts. Printing companies have a large library of fonts but not all of them. If you purchase or download a font for your artwork you should always include it with the artwork when handing it over to your printer. There are many different types of software but we will mention Adobe Photoshop®. If you are in Photoshop go to your top menu: Layer/Type/Convert to Shape and that will convert your font to "art" or "rasterize" your font. This will help you to avoid font issues.

4. What format should I hand my artwork in? Printers nowadays can accept many formats: .tiff, .jpeg or even in .psd format (Adobe PhotoShop® Document). This leads into number 5.

5. Once handing in your file in .psd format make sure that you clean out your layers or "junk" layers. Too many unneeded layers can cause possible mistakes during production of the print.

6. If and whenever possible hand in a "hard copy" of what your final should be. A "hard copy" is a color or black and white version of your print, not necessarily to scale, printed from your home printer and is given to the printer as a visual reference of what the final should look like.

7. This may sound simple but is very important. Once you pickup your printed piece from a printer or receive the package, check what it looks like right away so you can take care of the problem at the print shop or call the printer right away for a correction. Imagine picking up your prints and driving 30 minutes back home to have to get right back in your vehicle and return to the print shop.

8. Ask the print shop what they can print. Every print shop has its limits and you should know them. In your art, you may have very thin lines and the printer or print shop should let you know if they can hold that thin line.

9. Know your "bleeds". If you are working on a project and you want the art to go off the page then that is a "bleed". If your format is 8x10 then you should work at least 8.5 x 10.5 because this will give you .25 all around in extra space. The printer needs that space because they print on large sheets and then trim them to your specified size.

10. Understand your finishes and materials. Printers have plenty of finishes you can get and knowing what it will look like is important and knowing what you want is key. The three major differences are gloss, semi gloss and matte. Depending what you want the final print to look like choose your finish wisely. Textured paper is another scope of finish and very important too. If you want a movie poster look then a semi gloss paper would be just fine. If you want a fine art look to your print then a matte on textured canvas material should suffice.

By George Vega - Art Director

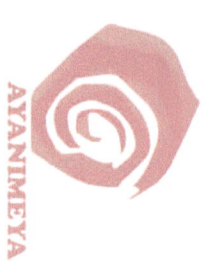

AYANIMEYA

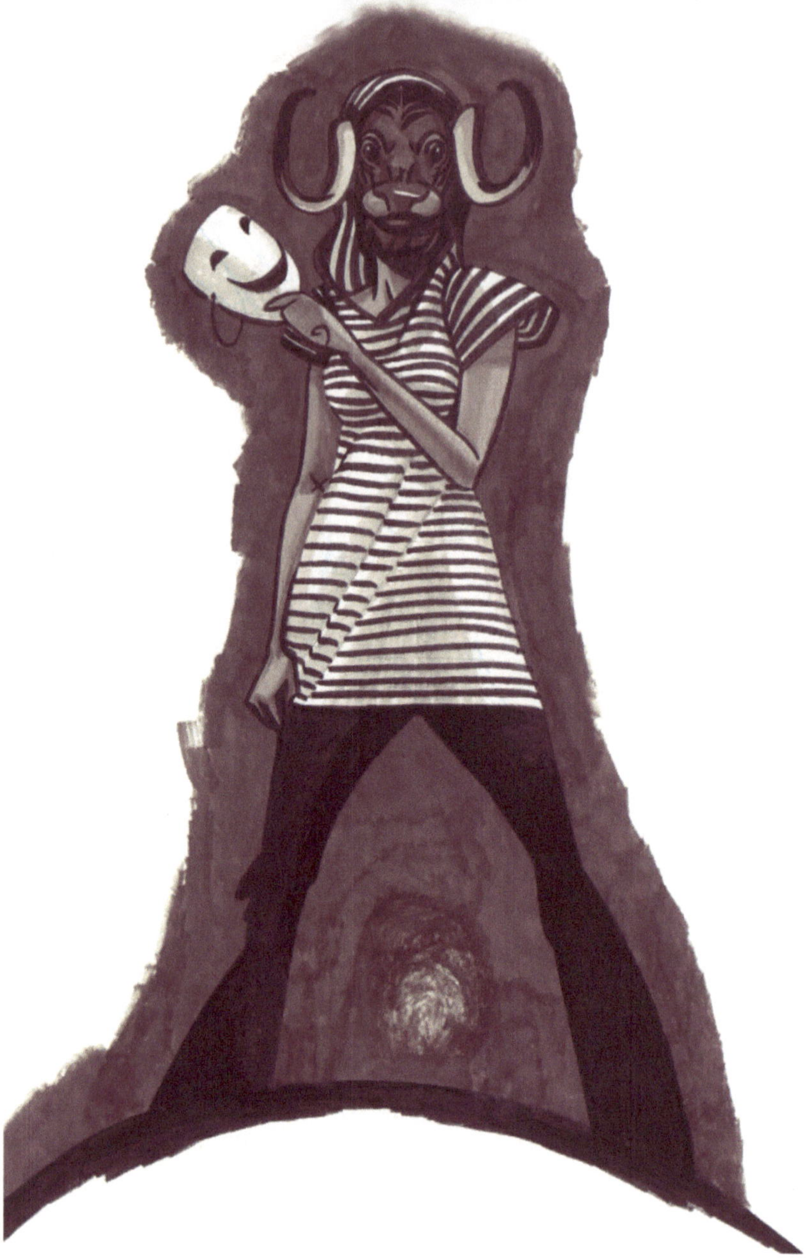

alina URUSOV *aka* Ayanimeya

Alina never really had higher aspirations than to make art, but if she found a magic lamp she reckons she'd ask to be turned into a mermaid.

Alina attended various art schools which helped in developing technical art skills but which mainly only provides food for reflection now that she sits at home making art for all sorts of companies.

She currently resides in Toronto Canada and hopes to continue to lead a friendly tree-loving existence without too many all-nighters. She has high hopes for her cat to, one day, make her obscenely rich.

Contact: web www.cloudypool.blogspot.com   e-mail alina_urusov@yahoo.com

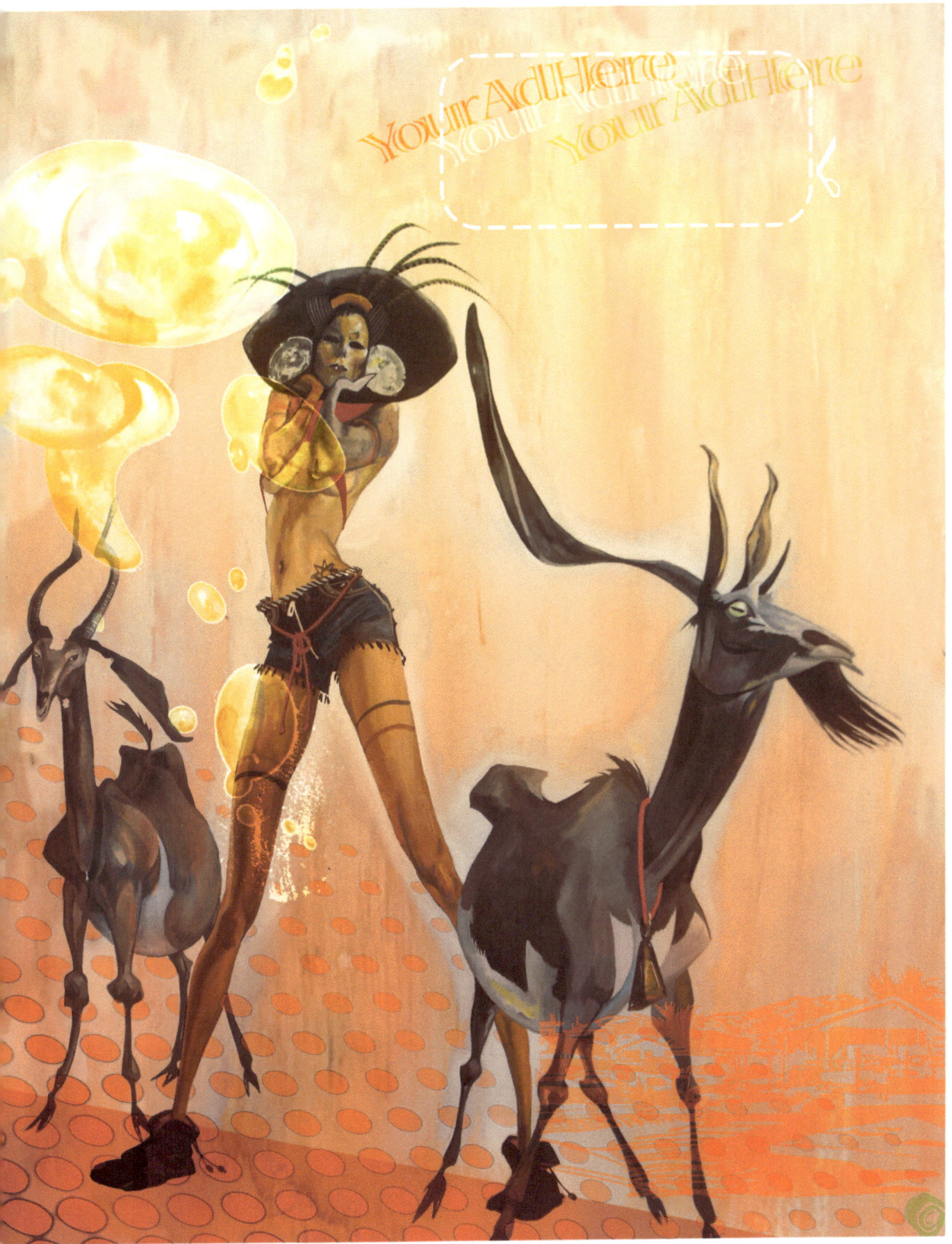

lly Goat

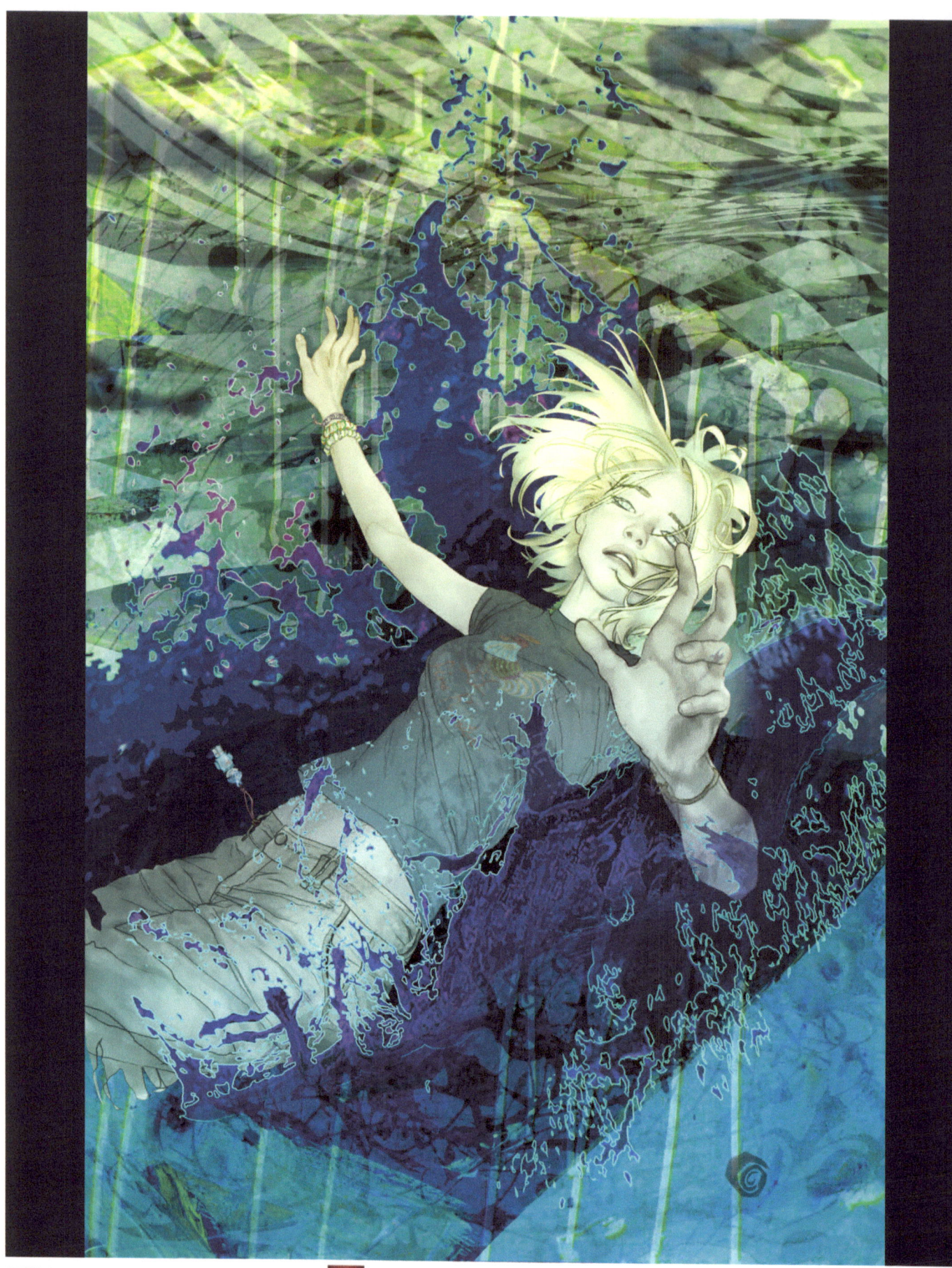

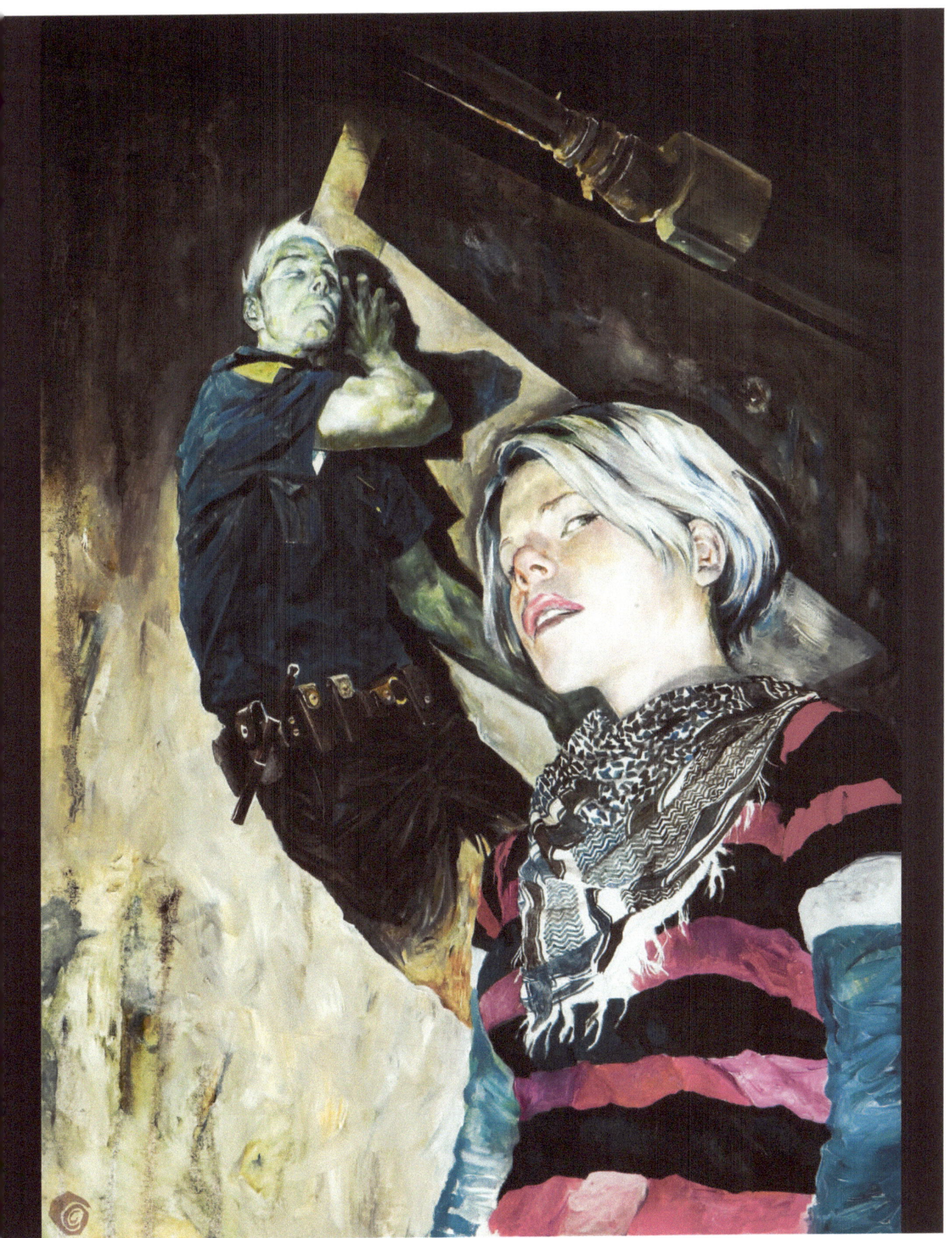

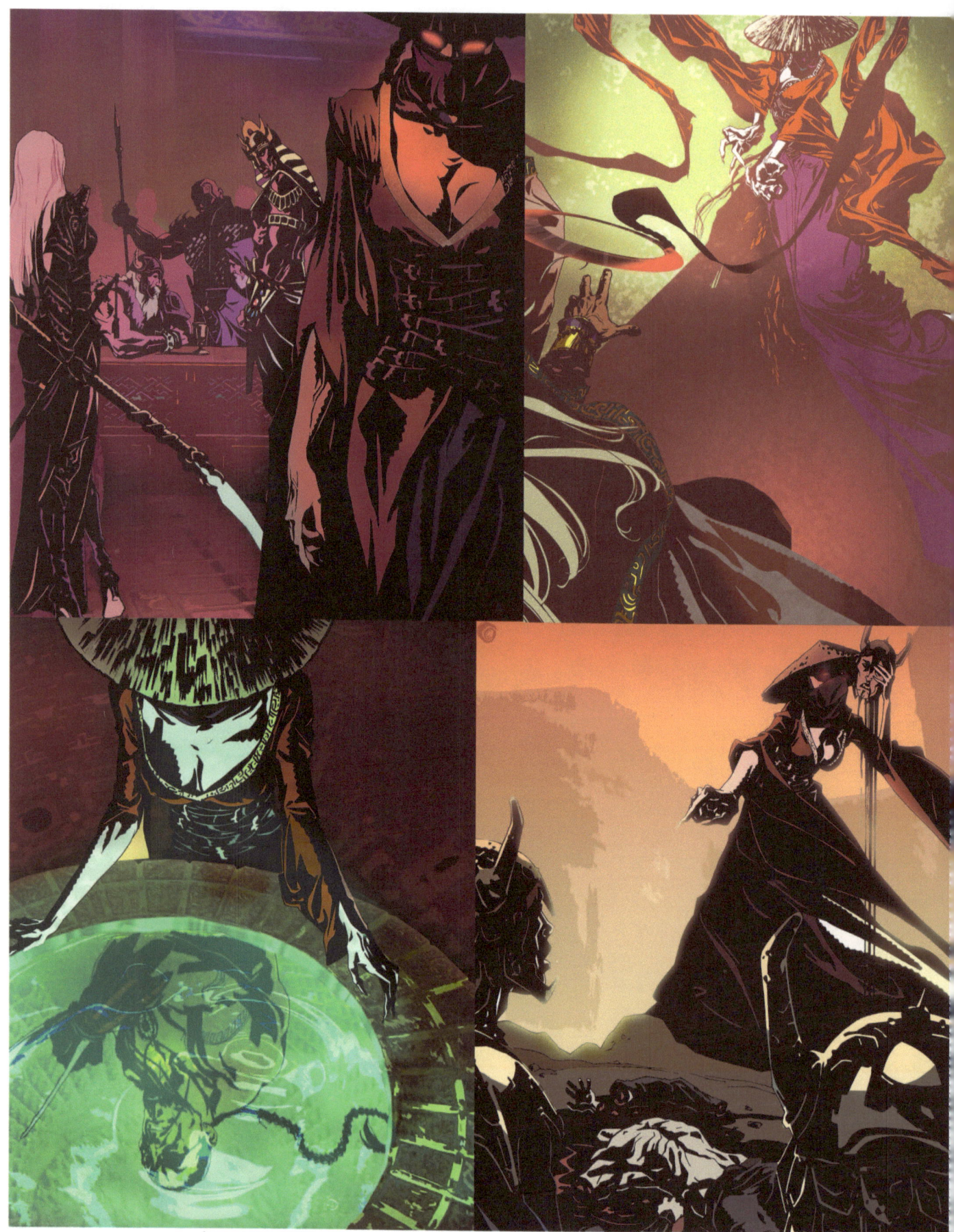

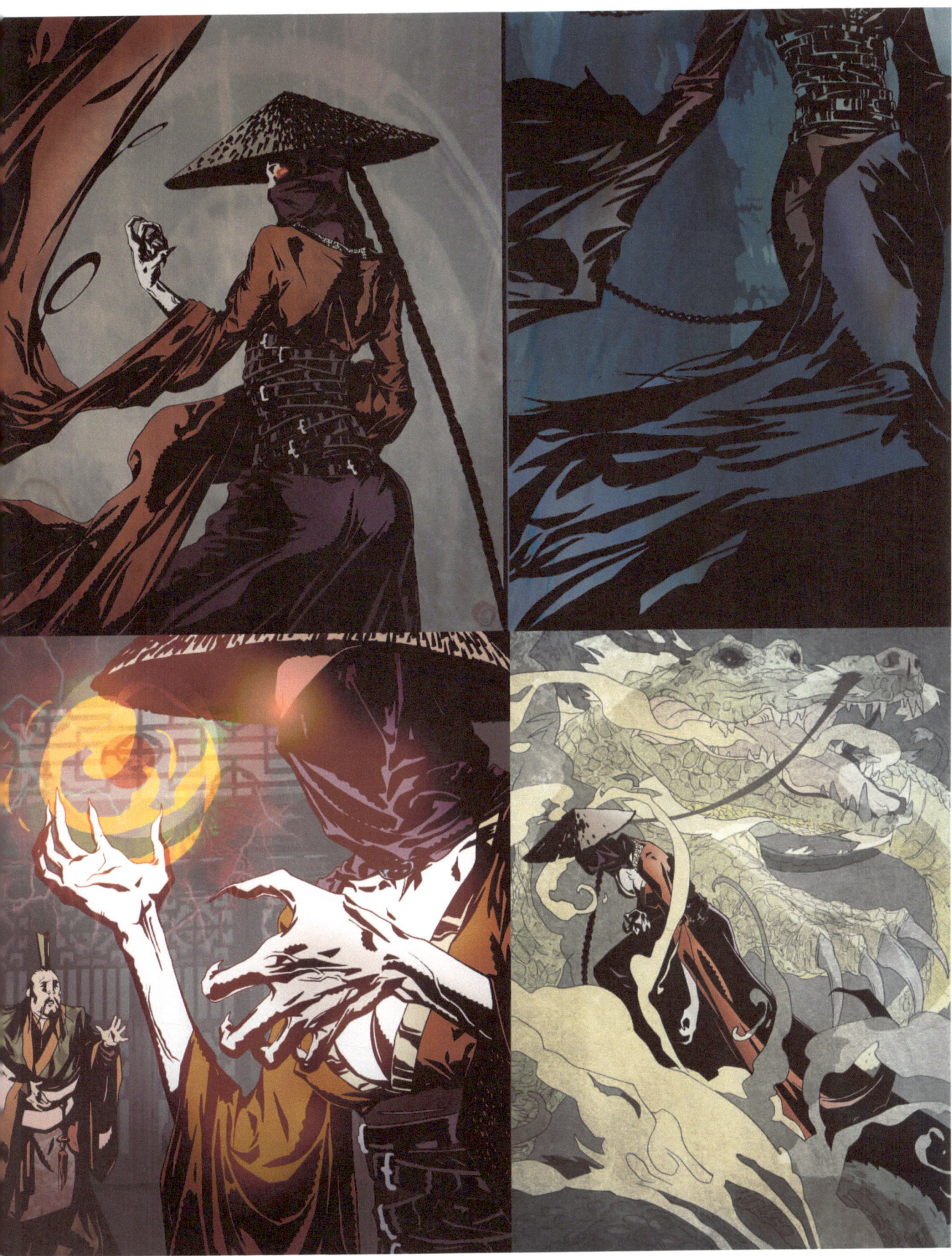

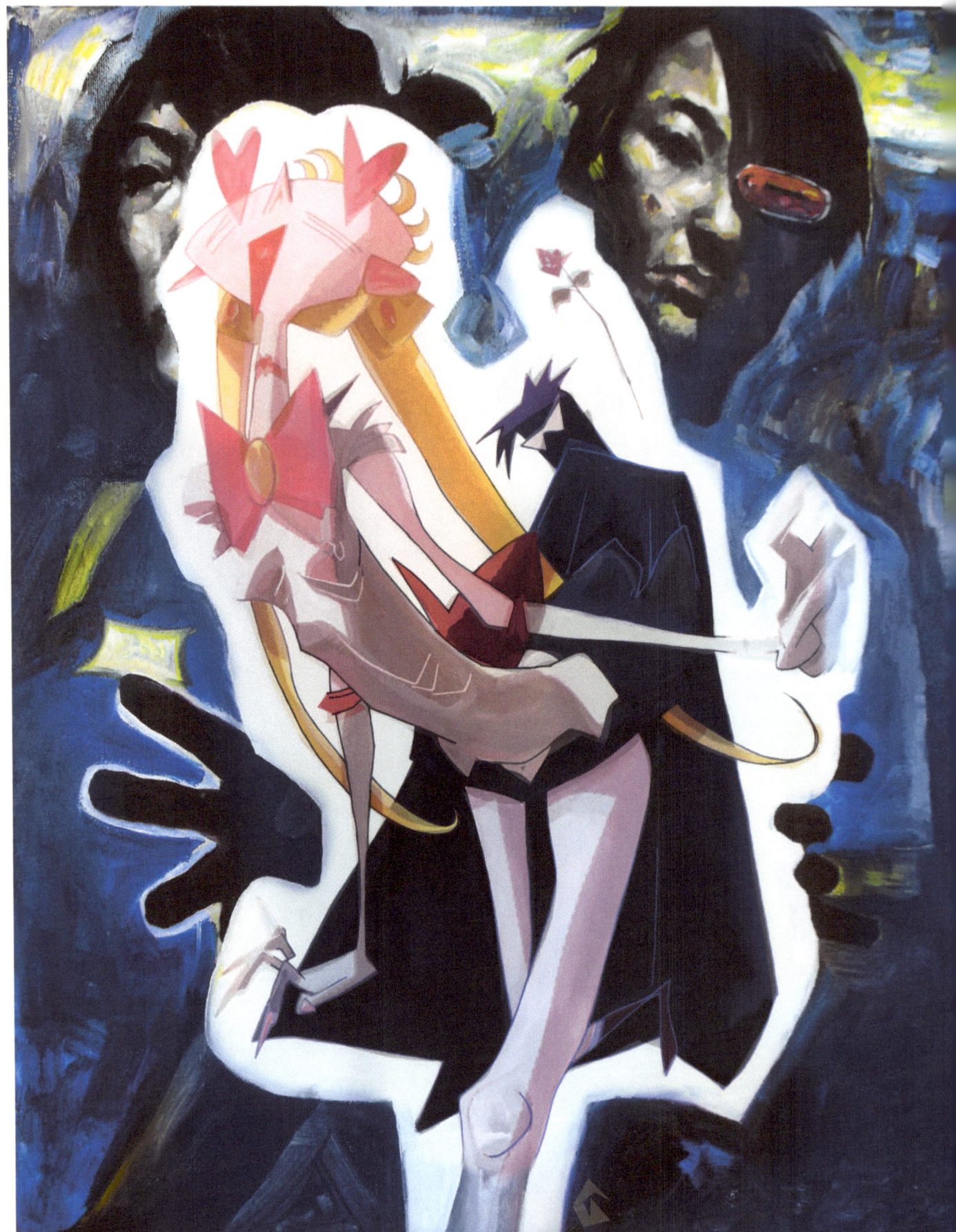

Sailor Moon

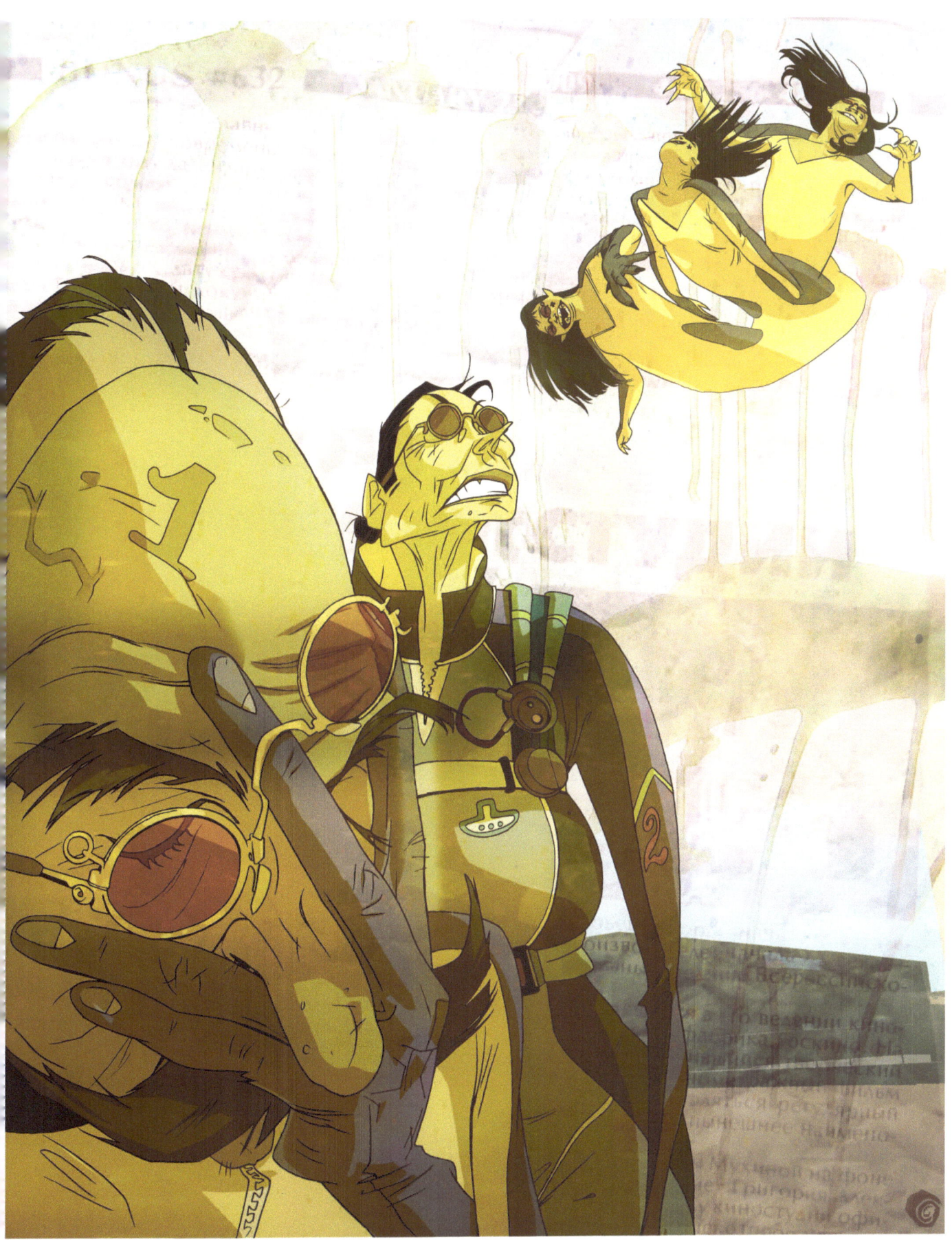

Yellow Family

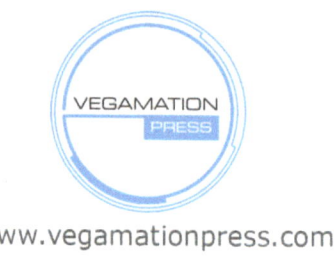

www.vegamationpress.com

VegamationPress publishes the newest and most outstanding artists. In today's industry it seems harder to be noticed in the art world and so we created a platform to show off the best.

INTRO DUCING

■ ■ ■

We would like to thank the artists that put so much hard work into this book and for their amazing original art. We would also like to thank the graphic designers and art directors that made this book happen.

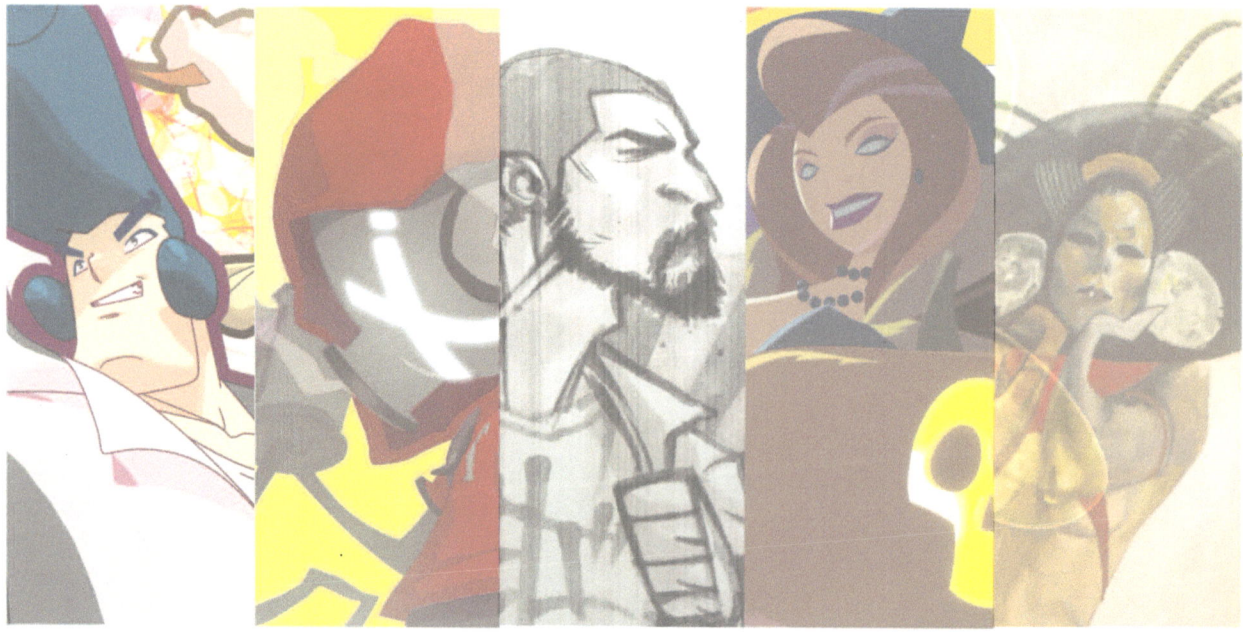